AF489957

2

Copyright ©2020 por Wendy Colón Nieves

Fotografía de portada: Jerica Colón

God with us

Wendy Colón Nieves

Content

Preface

Yes, that's right: God with us! An experiential reality evidenced in the testimony of more than a dozen women of God, from a Latin context, who knew how to say, "Here I am, Lord" and took steps of faith and courage. Wendy Colón is a passionate servant of God, committed, dedicated, sensitive, supportive, and a woman of prayer, who has experienced the reality of God in her daily life.

In God, with us, you will find an interesting, entertaining, emotional, and genuine compilation of experiences. In a masterful way, Wendy has managed to record this series of testimonies of Latin women who have believed in God and have been willing to respond to serve in His mission. Women who have faced great challenges, obeyed their call, confident that the One who called them, also accompanied them in every step. Some were single, others married and some with children. It distributes their stories with experiences in the field, describing their calling process and making a theological reflection of what these women have lived. It is constructed in such a way that once you start reading, it will capture your attention and you will want to keep going until you finish.

I met Wendy in the late 1990s as part of AMIES' short trips to Venezuela. It struck me that she was participating in the trip to the Waraos in her capacity as an agronomist, to teach them how to plant on the top of the water. For me it was impressive, but for her, it was a great challenge and for them, it was a whole process; very curious indeed. You will learn about it in the development of her testimony. We shared on several occasions during her leadership as mission's president of the First Christian Church (Disciples of Christ) in Vega Alta, Puerto Rico, and together with her pastor, she promoted with passion and dedication the missionary vision of her local church. Later I saw her develop in the ministry of Bible translation with great passion and zeal, now in the leadership of international character. Wendy excelled in such a way that God led her to serve in the Ibero-American missionary movement, leading Women in Missions as part of the COMIBAM International team.

There is no one better than Wendy to fill this void, this need to compile and record all this wealth of lived experiences. She has known firsthand the significant contribution of Latina women in extending the kingdom of God, particularly among the least reached with the gospel. The struggles and difficulties they face in overcoming the obstacles, the prejudices of the culture, and standing firm in their calling. How valuable and inspiring each experience is for others to be motivated to respond as well, for the harvest is still plentiful... God with us was needed. I love your expression that, through these stories, "we are going to see the feminine face of God in the missions".

I take this opportunity to share a concern with the church today. Responding to God's call continues to be essential to fulfill God's mission. And we are the church of the 21st century, with more resources and possibilities than the church had in the past 20 centuries. It is good that this book contains experiences of women responding to the call from the 1980s to the present day. I answered God's call in 1979. At that time, there were no missionary congresses, no mission schools, and no Latin mission agencies. God called me while I was still a college student. In '83 I traveled to Peru, with a one-way ticket, to serve in church planting, sent by my local church, the Assemblies of God. I knew nothing about missions or Peru, but the Holy Spirit guided and protected me every step of the way, allowing me to raise up the work in Arequipa and help raise up another one in Puerto Maldonado. I had finally managed to adapt and wanted to continue for many years when surprisingly God called me to return to Puerto Rico. "You alone can do a lot, but with 10 you can do more and I need you to teach others," were the Lord's words. It was not easy to leave Peru, but obeying will always be the best. So, I returned to Puerto Rico in 1987 to start El-Shaddai Ministries, which in '95 became AMIES and later led me to start WEC Latino. Since then, God has called me to serve in missionary mobilization.

Responding to God's call is much more than just going to the front lines. It is a determination to obey, to fulfill God's purpose, no matter the cost. Certainly, many walk to the altar, but they do not pass from the altar, and God wants us to pass from the altar to world missionary work. God continues to call workers to the harvest. And He continues to be God with us. To respond is to obey and to obey we must be intentional. To take action steps, guided by God's Holy Spirit. It will never be easy, but it will always be the best. The safest place to be is in God's will. "If God is for us, who is against us?" (Romans 8:31 RV60) I congratulate my beloved sister and friend Wendy for answering God's call for this project that will bless many. Each testimony in God with Us will make you identify with these women (many of whom I know personally) and make you want to do more for missions. In this time of crisis due to the coronavirus pandemic, this book is a motivational and inspirational resource. Thank you, Wendy, for blessing us with your testimony and that of all these brave women of God whom I also congratulate and bless.

Rev. Luz Esther Cádiz Arroyo
WEC International Missionary
President-Founder AMIES-PR
Ambassador COMIBAM International

Dedication

"And whatever you do or say, do it as true followers of the Lord Jesus Christ, and give thanks to God the Father for what Christ has done for you. "

Colossians 3:17 NASB

I definitely have to dedicate this book to God and thank Him for the opportunity He has given me to do this project. But a project of God in the hands of a human being is only possible through prayer and intercession. And it is to the intercessors to whom I dedicate this book, to the missionaries invisible to many on earth, but present before the throne of the King, in the continuous audience for all his servants.

I want to dedicate this book to all those who have been my intercessors, a faithful group of my church that since I said yes to missions have been committed with me to travel with their prayers to every mission that God has entrusted to me. God has been with me in the field, but He has been with them in the bedroom attending to their cries for me, my family, and ministry.

But especially, I want to dedicate this book to Olivia Jaime de Serrano, a Salvadoran sister that God gave me. She is a powerful intercessor in God, a woman committed not only to God but also to his servants and handmaids, like me. The King has given her an audience every time she has come before Him to cry out for me on many occasions.

I thank God for her life and family; she and her husband have carried me in prayer for a long time. They have opened the doors of their home to host me, and this is a gift, the gift of hospitality. Olivia has treated me like a sister, even though I am so different from her, that is another gift, love. God has used his children to give me tokens of love and affection, which for me reflects the sincere love that God has placed in Olivia and her family for me.

Thank you, a thousand thanks, Olivia, for letting God use you, showing me that we may be far away physically, but in God we are close. Thank you for holding me up at times when I have felt frustrated, hurt, and sad; for challenging me to believe that God has called me to break down strongholds of the enemy, to accompany me on that walk.

Thank you, thank you a thousand times. I remain infinitely committed to you because you have obeyed God and prayed for me, you have been a faithful servant.

Introduction

Sitting in a hammock (or chinchorro as they call it in some countries) in front of a beautiful beach and under the pleasant shade of a palm tree resting, God spoke to her heart. God was there with her, as He has walked with her since she met Him. She was reading the Bible and admiring the scenery. There she began to wonder, how can more people recognize Him, how can they know Him more and better? She began to think of the many ways she could talk about God and let others know of His sacrifice, but suddenly a small coconut fell in front of her, oh, it was in one of the palm trees and she had not seen it.

Just as she had not seen that fruit, many of us, brother or sister who have this book in your hands, are unaware of the many missionaries and in particular, many Latin women, who are serving God in many countries in creative ways to carry the message, inspired by our Creator God. He accompanies them, inspires them, and supplies them with everything they need to fulfill their great commission.[1]

This book is intended to raise awareness of the work that some of these women do, their struggles, but also their victories, which could not be listed here. May they know how God calls Latina women to the field and may they recognize God's presence in them and their ministries; not only

---

[1] This is how God put it on the author's heart to write this book.

manifesting Himself but also directing them and inspiring the strategies for each place. To God be the glory!

In the first part, you will find short but true stories of Latina women who have served or are serving somewhere in the world, in non-traditional roles in the field, but all to reach one more for Christ and make His name known. Stories of struggles, of processes, that God used not only to bring lives to His feet through them but also to work in them. We are going to see the feminine face of God in missions. They are faces and life stories of resilient Latina women, who not only speak to the world with their words but also with their daily life experiences, showing the world that God walks with them daily.

The people in Latin America have learned to survive in regions where the economic and social crisis are indescribable; they are accustomed to develop strategies to survive and sustain their families in the midst of these crisis. This has been added as an advantage to the Latin women that go out to the field because they carry a baggage of experiences lived in their own countries that allow them to adapt more quickly to the mission fields that are difficult and that live social and economic situations very similar to those of Latin America. So, we see how, in spite of so many situations, the Latin women respond to the call to service in the field in spite of whatever situation they are living in. So, in the second part of the book I want to share with you how some of them were called.[2]

---

[2]In some cases, pseudonyms and names of countries other than the one in

In writing these life stories of Latina missionaries, their testimonies, and their personal experiences serving in mission fields, I began to reflect on the theology that without realizing it, we practice daily in the fields we serve. So, in the third part of the book, I share some of these reflections, thinking about the fields where these women are and the theology that they live there.

Something special for you who have been called to the field..., for me?

The mission road is just that, a road where you can find freshwater to drink, green pastures to lie down and rest, beautiful landscapes that nature and God offer us. But there will also be some stones on that road that can make it difficult to walk, stumbling blocks that can cause sprains, and even dangerous animals that, willingly or unwillingly, can hurt us or try to stop our step. But we must be sure of one thing: He walks with us and from the moment we are called He accompanies us in everything. I know that this is the experience of many women who are on the road and Amapola de la Peña [3] could not have expressed it better when telling us about his experience, which I am including here...

"Since I was a child, I have heard about Psalm 23, for it is a very well-known Psalm, both by believers and non-believers. Some have their Bibles in their homes open to that Psalm, but perhaps very few have experienced its true

---

which these women serve are used for the safety of the women, their agencies and the church in that place.

[3] Pseudonym

meaning. God in His grace manifested Himself to me in a special way allowing me to experience the meaning of this Psalm where I learned more about the One who cares for me, guides me, and protects me.

"When I lived in China, one of my friends invited me to join her on a field day, which included hiking and possibly climbing a high mountain with a group of friends. I was very excited to go with her because I wanted to have the opportunity to share the gospel with her. The excitement kept me from remembering that I had always been afraid of heights. I was thinking only of the opportunity to share with my friend. So, without much thought, I agreed to go with her. When the day arrived, I was prepared with my climbing clothes and a large backpack containing everything I thought I would need for the day: water, food, a blanket to sit on the ground, among many other things. The backpack was a bit heavy, but I didn't think anything of it at the time. When we arrived at the place where the hike would begin, the bus dropped us off there and would pick us up at the same place in the afternoon. We started the hike in a valley, there were no mountains in that area, no obstacles that could affect us. As we progressed along the road, it became steeper and, in my opinion, dangerous. I thought about how difficult it would be to return to the starting point. Mountains began to appear and one higher than the last. They were difficult to climb. I began to see how far there was to go, and how difficult the road looked. Then, I stopped and thought I could not continue. The path looked harder and higher and higher. I thought I couldn't make it. Whew! And the weight of the backpack kept me from moving forward.

Suddenly, the leader of the group, who noticed my difficulty in climbing, came to my side, took my backpack, and gave me his stick so that I could support myself and continue. He reassured me with his gesture, but also with his words, he assured me that I could make it, that he would be by my side, and that he would not abandon me, that I only had to lean on him. In this way, with the help of the leader, although with difficulty, I continued up the mountain until I reached the top. To my surprise, this portion of the path became much easier and then I was able to continue without needing help, although the leader always remained close by.

We arrived at a beautiful place full of streams, trees, different types of flowers, and even some sheep and goats. It seemed like we were very close to heaven, and we spent the rest of the day there. I was able to share the gospel with my friend and sow the seed because, although she did not accept Christ as her Savior at that moment, she did at a later time. We then descended without the need for help. The experience made me reflect on various aspects of the Christian life and helped me to understand the meaning of Psalm 23 when it says: "The Lord is my shepherd; I shall not want. He makes me to lie down in green pastures: he leadeth me beside the still waters. He will comfort my soul; He will guide me in paths of righteousness for His name's sake...Thy rod and thy staff, they comfort me."

I felt as if I had lived this psalm. The group leader made me see God as my shepherd, my helper, my protector. The one who is faithful, the one who protects us, guides us, and takes us by the hand to places where we can rest. The one who comforts and encourages us. The One who is faithful, who promised that He would always be with us every day until the end and who promised that He would never leave us nor forsake us. It led me to reflect on the fact that we must lay aside every weight and that which is not important or essential in our Christian life (Hebrews 12:1b). Although the backpack contained things that were important for the walk-in my opinion, it also contained other things that I discovered were not essential and that prevented me from moving forward and reaching the goal. I understood that, just as the group leader was with me all the way and took my burden so that I could continue, Jesus carries our burdens and is with us always. I could see how important it is to keep our eyes on Jesus and not on the circumstances or what is around us (Hebrews 12:2). When we look at the circumstances and how difficult the road is we become afraid, we think we can't get there and sometimes we want to turn back. Circumstances often make us see our weaknesses, our inadequacy, and not the greatness of God, what He can and wants to do in our lives and in the lives of those to whom He has sent us. God reaffirms His faithfulness to all of us who are called to serve Him."

The Lord is my shepherd, I lack nothing.
He makes me lie down in green pastures,
he leads me beside quiet waters,
He refreshes my soul.
He guides me along the right paths
for his name's sake.
Even though I walk
through the darkest valley,
I will fear no evil,

for you are with me;
your rod and your staff,
they comfort me.
(Psalm 23:1-4, New International Version)

God with us

Why God with us? And not so many names came up as alternatives. Simply because this is a book of God... God manifested in many ways calling, accompanying, empowering, and working; in and through Latina women who have said "Yes, Lord, here I am."

God is using Latinas to impact the lives of women, men, indigenous people, Muslims, immigrants, refugees, gypsies, women at risk, theology students, in short, impacting communities through them; God showing himself to them and to the world, in a myriad of ways: in the provision, in healings, in open doors, in the diversity of creation, in faithfulness, in his care and protection, in the smile of the people who find him and receive him.

"God with us" is a recognition of the God that the missionaries see in the communities that receive them, but also in the organizations and churches that send them. It is the God that they see working in the hearts of the people who feel a call. "God with us", is just one statement of the many ways in which women like Siris, have known the God who sustains us, sustains us, and hears our cry, for His Glory and Honor.

18

God walks with us...before, during, and after serving Him.

"It happened that while they were talking and arguing among themselves, Jesus himself drew near, and walked with them." Luke 24:15 (RVR1960)

God walks with us when we are happy, but also in the midst of our sadness, confusion, pain, and even anger. The Emmaus walkers did not immediately realize that He was with them. Sadness did not allow them to recognize His presence, but there He was walking with them. As happened to these walkers, many times in missions, or in the midst of God's process of preparing us to serve in other places, we experience moments of pain and confusion. But He wants us to remember that, if we are serving in the field, He is walking with us. May we remember that He called us to prepare to go out into the field, and when we are experiencing great pain, He walks with us, as He walked with Clare in the following story.[4]

"At 1:30 in the afternoon, on February 27, 2006, everything that represented security, collapsed little by little with a single phone call. Behind the phone was my sister's broken, clipped voice: "Clara, they killed my daddy!" That morning full of clouds and cold in Bogota, with a 27-day-old baby girl and in the absence of my beloved husband Jorge, who

---

[4] Clara, missionary in Alicante, Spain for 6 years.

was out of town for his work, I watched as my oldest son Juan Felipe, only three years old, tried to understand the moment. The clouds and the cold outside tucked me inside, the call tore at my heart and soul.

We already knew about the danger my father was in at that time due to some threats, but we always consoled ourselves thinking that there was a safety frame, and told ourselves, "Nothing is NOT going to happen." But yes, it did happen. Uncertainty and pain that I had never felt before flooded me. Although one knows that at some point death will come, one never expects it in that way. Many times, we think that as Christians we are immune, that this kind of thing cannot happen to God's children. We forget that we are in this world full of afflictions. Believer or not, we are exposed to suffer the consequences of human deterioration, evil, and sin of this fallen world that affect everything.[5]

The guerrillas came with a whole arsenal and arrived very organized to Los Gabrieles, a recreational center in Rivera Huila, where my father was born and served with all his heart along with eleven other people, as councilmen of that

---

[5]*"All things happen in the same way to all; one and the same event befalls the righteous and the wicked; the good, the clean and the unclean; the one who sacrifices, and the one who does not sacrifice; as to the good, so to the one who sins; the one who swears, as to the one who fears the oath. This evil is among all that is done under the sun, that one and the same event befalls all, and also that the heart of the sons of men is full of evil and folly in their heart during their lifetime; and after this they go to the dead."* Ecclesiastes 9:2-3 New International Version

place. The guerrillas had a clear objective, to kill the town councilors, who offered confidence to their current government. They got out of their truck, and the first shots rang out. My father could not run, he could not defend himself, nor could he get up from his chair, because he had had surgery on his spine a month ago and in order to walk, he had to use a walker. We believe that he was one of the last to die and surely, he was the witness who witnessed the death of his companions. The bullets went through his arms, his torso, his neck, and finally his head.

Maybe people wonder if it is difficult and painful. And yes, it is. It is something that sadly unites those of us who have lost someone, especially through armed conflict. I confess that I wanted to know what happened in my father's last seconds, what he said, what he thought, what he did, or just try to understand the why and what for. Surely some people think we shouldn't ask God that, but it's unavoidable. I thought it was a way to heal my wounds. I thought surely that God was there, of course, there was. To unbelievers, it will probably sound ridiculous, but to me, it was real to think that way. It was the only way I could think that something meaningless could make sense.

This situation wounded my faith, a faith that I carried wounded for a while, as the questions kept coming up: How could I, being a Christian, live through something like this; couldn't God have warned me; couldn't God have defended my father; couldn't God have done something? I knew I was not a perfect Christian; I knew I was under his hand as a daughter, but I waited for his answers to all my questions. However, they did not come.

In those years of intense struggle within me, the Lord worked deeply and unwaveringly in His purpose to heal my wounds with the most tender care, so that the wounds would not open, but simply close and heal. In the midst of that healing process, my husband and I received our missionary call. We were sent as missionaries to Spain, to work in the Amor Fraternal Love Church[6] with Pastors Cesar and Patricia. We were there for six years serving and helping with all the desire in our hearts to please the Lord.

While there, my third daughter, Isabella, was born, bringing great joy to my heart. In the midst of that joy, God spoke to me about my wounded faith. What!? He pointed out to me something that remained there, kept as if in a chest of old objects, hidden in the attic of an old house. How tremendous! I had to face reality with its own name, so, in the middle of the labyrinth of my thoughts and questions, I found a way out, to heal, yes, to heal my wounded faith to reach the point of NOT blaming God anymore. Yet, He continued to walk with me in the midst of this healing process.

*After this time in Spain, we returned to Colombia, welcomed by the Church **Puente Largo**[7] and by our pastors*

---

[6] *"Above all, love each other deeply, because love covers over a multitude of sins."* (1 Peter 4:8 NIV)

22

Luis and Alexandra who had adopted us as their missionaries. It was there that I realized that I had the key to a lost door and that was to be able to forgive my father's victimizers. I know you may be thinking: Oh, Lord, how can a Christian of so many years and a missionary live with that? Well, yes, it is just like the battles you fight every day until you finally win the victory over the war. I was in the middle of that battle trying to overcome the bruises and bruises in my heart that got worse every time I saw the victimizers who continued to do harm in the midst of the peace agreement that Colombia signed in 2016.

Then you will say to me: "How long can it take for someone to truly forgive? It is true that some things are easier to forgive than others. It also depends on our willingness to decide to let go and let go of the offense. In my experience the sooner I decide the better, to prevent resentment from advancing and turning into bitterness, which I consider to be a sin. So I made the decision to forgive every word or every attitude that I knew or imagined that the perpetrators expressed to the victims. So it was that on the 12th anniversary of my father's death, the "tow truck" arrived that could tow my load and take it away, God walked with me on this hard journey of forgiveness with a lot of patience and love. (You will find out later what happened)."

God walks with us in solitude...

---

[7] He returned to Colombia to the Puente Largo Church, where his road to forgiveness and healing was also long, but there he discovered his ability to forgive with the help of God and his pastor, the angel of the church.

"I will not leave you until I have fulfilled all that I have promised you" (Genesis 28:15), has been the Word that has given Mirely the certainty that Jesus has walked with her in her journey. Jesus has walked with her in her learning and adapting to a new culture, where the treatment of women is different, where the language, food, and personal relationships are also different. But in everything God has been with her. He accompanied her in the plane she took to reach the mountain in the state of Humla in Nepal, in a flight between the Himalayan mountains. He accompanied her on her eight-hour walk for two days, making her way to the village where she would work. He accompanied her and kept her while she slept in huts, without bathing for several days. Yes, Jesus has certainly walked with her for fifteen years in the mission field.

God has been with her not only on these roads, but in every challenge, in every moment of fear, and in her loneliness. Yes, in her loneliness, because in spite of having arrived at the field with her husband, there were moments in which loneliness was present with different faces. They were faces of longing for the familiar, for the cultural, for the known, for her church, for the pastor, and even for the language, things that make us forget at times that God walks with us. These are things and experiences that blind us as they blinded the walkers of Emmaus.

"Loneliness, loneliness, and loneliness. When you arrive you immediately feel it. When you make friends, it is strong. I can't imagine how it must feel for those who go out to the country as singles, if it was so strong for me, I have no idea how it is for them. You start from scratch in the country

where you arrive. You have to gain the trust of the pastors and ministers there. You don't have your family and church close to you, to embrace you and accompany you physically. Holidays and celebrations are different in the country. For example, Christmas Day in Nepal is an everyday workday that is not celebrated. Seeing videos and photos of family and friends celebrating it with the food you love, ah, how sad it is! Scenes like that somewhat aggravate that feeling of longing and loneliness. I remember in November 2005 was my sister's wedding. I was unable to attend to accompany her on that special day. Needless to say, I cried inconsolably all that day for not being able to be with her, but God comforted me.

I thank God for the technology that today helps us to see each other despite the distance. But when I arrived in the country, I could only communicate with my parents once a month, 15 minutes by phone, because communication was very expensive. Even so, despite having the technology now, it is not the same to talk in person and receive a hug. It is painful, seeing your family members growing up, celebrating events and holidays without you, or seeing your church singing and receiving the Word of God in your native language. Wow! It's really hard.

I remember during my first year in the field I cried every day. I missed my family and siblings so much. In spite of the loneliness and challenges, I did not become paralyzed; I continued God's work there. We began to make friends. Seven months into our stay in India, we moved to Nepal and started all over again. Other friends came; we celebrated our holidays and continued to work. We felt that God was always present.

It is difficult for a minister to get a person with whom you can talk about sensitive situations. Imagine being in another country and having no one you trust to talk to. This is how you learn to depend completely on God. He is the one who is with you every step of the way; he comforts you at night and is present in difficult situations. He is the only one who knows things that you don't tell your family and friends, so they don't worry." (Mirely)

Walking in God...only by his grace

"Grace is God's attitude of looking at us in our lost and helpless condition but looking at us with love. It is with that same love that I firmly believe God looked at me to lead me to the fulfillment of my life's purpose.

Walking with God is different from walking in God. You could say that you walk with God and live by his principles, set his priorities, and do his will, or you could also say that there are certain rules with which you do not agree. But to walk in God is to walk in the Principles of the Kingdom, accepting His priorities over yours (or mine). To walk in God is to go through the processes that will lead your life in victory and into God's purpose.

I needed to write all of the above to delve into the most important thing...character and intimacy. In the midst of all that God has allowed me to experience until before traveling to

Brazil, I could say it was my old self. A self-full of pride, selfishness, pride, resentments, vanities, and insecurities. After leaving Brazil, it is me now, totally transformed. Brazil was for my life a land of blessings, training, growth, faith, and obedience. I have always been intimated with God and He has revealed Himself to my life in an amazing way, but in Brazil, I lived my time of greatest growth.

My story of change began in volunteer work in the mission field. I was collaborating with an NGO[8] I was in charge of developing development projects for Asia. The first day I started my work, I met a pastor who I will call Roberto (not his real name). Never in my life had I met such a cultured and educated person. Being a pastor, he had a pleasant manner with others, always with a smile on his face and I believe he knew how to deal with all personality types. When I met him, I said to myself..... I want to be like him! This servant was my role model. I think we all probably have someone as an example that helps us to strive to be better.

In me, there was a resistance to drastic changes that did not allow me to grow; I was reluctant to bend. When you are in the field, you have to learn to deal with people, regardless of their nationality and culture. You have to learn to adapt to a new environment where you will be away from family and friends, and where you will often feel lonely. It requires learning to communicate through the native language

---

[8] NGOs are acronyms for non-governmental, non-profit organizations that carry out activities of social interest. They do not depend on the government.

of the place and knowing how to listen. But above all, it is learning to love and to serve.

To love and to serve are two important factors for a change. When one loves, says 1st Corinthians 13, "one suffers all things, believes all things, hopes all things, endures all things". Learning to be patient like Pastor Roberto was a great miracle for me. I learned to see the love in people and with that, I began to see the selfishness in me disappear. I learned to say "yes" to the Lord when it was necessary to part with money, clothes, shoes, books, and more because material things can become our worst enemy.

It took many years to develop the ability to give my heart without expecting anything in return. Selfishness was gone from my heart. When I understood that only by His love and only by His grace were inner transformations achieved, doors began to open. People began to recognize that I had a calling and a ministry. People hungry and thirsty for the word sought me out to receive advice, a hug, a word of encouragement, and to know who Jesus is." (Jenny Marcela Cuadros)

God walks with us and opens the way...

And that's how Carolina saw it one day on her way back from El Salvador to Japan. This is how God walked with her through the airport, opening the way for her on her route to service in the mission field:

"I was traveling with a "space condition" ticket in August, high season. I took the plane from El Salvador and made my stopover in the United States. There, the flights were already very full. I missed my next connection to Japan. The airline staff suggested that I not wait until the next day on the same route, because the same thing would happen, so I had better change my itinerary, and so I did. Then I went to get my bags in the cargo section. I didn't know at the time that when I went down to the cargo section, I would be outside the airport.

In order to access the airport again, I asked the front desk to print my ticket. It was there where, at almost ten o'clock at night, I was notified that the computer system had crashed and that they would not be able to print my ticket. The only solution was to contact the person who sold me the ticket in El Salvador. I was worried because my flight would be leaving in an hour. I immediately sent a message to the person who sold me the ticket, as well as another message to a prayer group, who immediately began to intercede for me.

After a while, I went back to the reception desk at the airport, and this time an elderly man who had just taken the other shift was there. I told him my situation and asked if he could print my ticket for me. His attitude of kindness, serenity, and peace was like having an angel in front of me helping me. He saw the system on the computer, did not tell me anything, just made a couple of calls, and went and printed my ticket which was in space condition. This allowed me to re-enter the boarding section of the airport. I went running through the aisles, as my flight would be leaving in a few minutes. But to my surprise, when I arrived at the gate lounge, it looked like a celebration. There was airplane food and drinks from the airline for the passengers because the plane had been delayed for an hour. Then my name was mentioned over the loudspeaker, and it was to ask me in which seat position I wished to travel. With a conditional ticket, one is not asked this question but is assigned one of the available seats. In every moment of this situation, I was able to experience the power of prayer together, God's favor and protection clearing my path." (Carolina)

God leads us to the right place. And yes, it is worth it

"Perhaps you want to know if I've ever wondered, is it worth all that I've done and how I've done it? Well, it was the morning of January 17, 2015, when I was in Boston, doing some presentations to invite churches to get involved in missions and visiting a colleague. With less than a week to return to Africa, there I was very happy to have shared a little over a month, about our projects and the progress of the work. That morning I was awakened by the terrible news of the terrorist acts that had occurred in the nation where I was serving. The day before and during that morning, the radical group Boko-Haram had allegedly entered from the neighboring country. More than sixty churches, at least four Christian schools, and some western businesses were burned; including the two Horizons churches, the ministry I serve with, and our elementary school. The group continued to make threats to wipe out missionaries in the country that weekend. Everything was really very confusing; chaos and fear reigned, and many questions arose in my head... I could not understand.

There was a whirlwind in my mind, why was God allowing all this, where was the effort and investment of more than twenty years? I remember that I cried a lot, with a mixture of helplessness, anger, and pain, as well as uncertainty about the state of my companions and friends. There was a sense of guilt in me for not being there with them.

I received instructions from the international leadership to postpone my return to Africa, and who knows whether to divert it to Venezuela... What?! To leave the camp abruptly, with so much to do and so few workers!!!!! At that moment I did not even think about the risks.

It was then that I asked myself: Is it worth it? I delayed my return to the field for three weeks, waiting to see what would happen. A week later, I went to Dallas to share in new churches about the projects and recent events. When I mentioned the country, many people didn't even know where it was or mistook it for another country. It was a great opportunity that God opened to make known these people so lacking and in need of God. In the following days, more people around the world joined in, not only to pray but also to cause a transformation in many senses.... Observing how quickly God responded, and how many people everywhere got involved and worked together to fulfill His plan to bless the nations, made me realize that the Lord always has me in the right place according to His perfect plan... and that, indeed, it IS WORTH IT!" *(Katiusca Ibarra)*

God walks with us and clears our doubts...that heal our self-esteem.

"I can tell you that I was surprised to realize that Jesus was walking with me in the streets of Venezuela to remove from my heart pain and restlessness that I carried with me. I am from Puerto Rico, a Caribbean Island, where most people speak loudly. I, in particular, can say that I grew up in a large family where everyone speaks at the same time and very loudly. That's what I learned, and, in addition, I have a very loud tone of voice. For a while, this was problematic and even embarrassing for me in missions. I have worked with many nationalities and with all kinds of people, and many times I was told to be quiet or told to lower my voice because they understood that I was shouting. Although for me, I was just talking, in my natural Caribbean tone. So many times, I was shushed or told to lower my voice that I began to feel bad, self-conscious, and even humiliated. Even if I lowered the volume of my voice, it was still loud. So, I tried to keep my voice low or I didn't speak at all because it was difficult to keep my voice low all the time.

But God showed up and walked with me. I was on a trip to serve as an agronomist to the Warao Indians in the middle of the jungle in Venezuela. I was returning with the missionary Peter, from the agricultural center to buy some materials that I needed. His comment surprised me, as he said to me, "Jesus must have had a very strong tone of voice, like yours." I looked up from the floor and said, "What?" He repeated, "That Jesus had to have had a very loud tone of voice, like yours." He continued, "Speaking from a boat in the

32

middle of the lake and from there preaching for all to hear without sound equipment, he definitely must have had to have had a loud voice." I kept thinking about his words, recognizing that they were not from the missionary. It was God walking with me and taking away that weight that others had placed on me.

During that trip and already in the jungle, the church began to fill up every night. One day the sound system had broken down and without it, we could not preach the message for everyone to hear. Without it, we could not preach the message for everyone to hear. Who do you think was the one who solved the problem? The one who spoke the loudest. That night I preached with all my voice and declared the wonders of God loudly and many accepted the Lord. He walked with me to make it clear to me that He had made me this way to serve Him just as I am." (Wendy)

God walks with us and gives us words of encouragement...

On the road of service to God things happen that we cannot explain or understand, but what we can be sure of is that He walks with us, and when He sees that we are about to faint, His words give us encouragement and sustain us. This is what has been happening to Elisabeta Diaz…

"Thanks to God's provision, in the month of June 2017, my husband and I traveled to the Balkans where God confirmed His call on our lives, to bring His message of salvation and love to the Roma (Gypsy) people of Tetovo, in Macedonia. We communicated to the pastors of our church in El Salvador what God showed us, and them and the rest of the church supported us.   We began a process of preparation with many "garage sales," visits to churches to seek their support and after two years, in the month of May 2019, we went out to the field. At that time the Lord began to speak to my heart, telling me that He would go before us (Deuteronomy 31:8). With that promise, we boarded a plane that took us from our "Thumbelina" (affectionate name for the Republic of El Salvador) to Spain where we spent three days.   Then we left for Turkey where we spent a terrible night at the airport with eight suitcases and two tired little ones of five and eight years old. The next day, early on May 25, we left on a short flight to Skopje, the capital of North Macedonia, where a loving team of cross-cultural workers awaited us. Thus began the greatest adventure of our lives. We spent a month in the city of Tetovo, getting to know the team and working together at the summer camp. In the month of July, we moved to the capital, to start our Macedonian language learning to get to know the culture. Unfortunately, at the end of August, we had to leave the country in a hurry, as my husband's visa had been rejected and the three months we were allowed as tourists were coming to an end.   We moved to the neighboring country of Albania, where we would make a second attempt to apply for the visa, as it had been rejected due to a recent change in the Macedonian laws. In theory, because of this small change, the process would not take long, and we would soon be able to return. But what we thought would be resolved in three weeks, took three months to resolve. The time in Albania was difficult. Our hearts were still burning for Macedonia. We received proposals to stay there, for, as you may know, the harvest is plentiful, and the laborers are always few. We prayed and the

Lord began to show us that we should stand firm in the call He had already given us.

When we managed to return to DOMMA (Macedonian for home), we continued with our language classes, and everything was falling into place. But in January 2020, we received the news that my husband's visa had been renewed for only six months. This meant that only he could stay in Macedonia, but at the end of the month, my children and I would have to leave the country again. Once again, we remembered to stand firm and made the decision. We were able to ask for help from a Kosovar pastor who found us an affordable apartment, with everything we needed. We thought that my husband, having his visa, would be able to visit us regularly. But surprise, only a couple of weeks had passed, when the world crisis of the Coronavirus hit us, with the closing of borders and mandatory quarantine for all. So, we began this time of forced separation, my husband in one country and me alone with my children in another. One day my husband told me: "God prepared you for this time with the women's ministry" and I believe he did because it has been a time in which I have experienced giving everything and even beyond my strength. I know there is a saying "God doesn't give you something you can't carry", but really, I believe there is no biblical support for that. On the contrary, we find more passages, where we see people being brought down beyond their strength and are only delivered by the power of God. The Second Letter to the Corinthians has brought us much consolation. One day the Lord took me to the first chapter, verses six through eleven. Later that day, my husband called me to read the same passage to me, for the Lord had taken him there also. It was very beautiful to see how our God unites us, despite the distance and comforts our hearts as if they were one. The Lord is molding me through this trial, and even though there are times when my faith is lacking and the trial is getting harder and harder, I know that Jesus promised, He would always be with me." [9]

Women who serve in missions are as human as anyone else and even knowing God's Word and believing in Him, and loving Him, there are times when disappointment knocks at the door, particularly when we have expectations of others who we believe think as we do. But God shows up and reminds us that everything is in His hands. Magdalena felt that disappointment for a moment...

"During my chairmanship in the missions committee of my church, I had the hope that a married couple would be in the ministry, and I thought they could be the ideal couple to continue in charge of the ministry when I was not there. After a while, I found out from them that they wanted to be in another ministry which made me very sad. One day one of the sisters in the church said to me, "Magdalena, you look bad; what happened to you?" I told her, "I am very sad and disillusioned, waiting for what is not going to happen." At that very moment another sister arrived and gave me a card with the word of God in Isaiah 41: 10, "Fear not for I am with you;

---

[9] At the time of writing this book, Elisabeta's husband was still in another country and sick with the coronavirus along with other ministers of God. After four months, he was reunited with his family. Let us pray for so many of God's servants who get sick in the fields.

be not dismayed, for I am your God who strengthens you; I will always help you, I will always uphold you with the right hand of my righteousness."

God turned a moment of disappointment and Magdalena's expectations and set His own, bringing to her remembrance that He was still in control.

God hears our prayer in the way of fear and danger...

Abigail[10] and his family recognized God in the peace He offered them in the midst of persecution and danger…

"Independence Day was approaching in Uzbekistan, and the situation for all the workers there began to change. The government had expelled about 90% of the workers working in the country. Since the beginning of the year, the government did not want to start renewing visas due to some "technical problems", they only offered people whose visas were expiring a permit to stay in the country while their process was being completed. When these permits began to expire, the government did not want to renew them or grant visas, so people had to leave the country. By the summer of that year, something alerted us all that the situation was not going to improve. Many workers who did have visas went to their countries on vacation and when they returned to the country they were not allowed to re-enter. It was chaos; families were deported from the airport without even being able to go home to retrieve some of their belongings. It was very sad and painful to hear how families we knew had not

[10] Pseudonym

been able to re-enter the country. Our children lost many of their friends. Every week we heard of a family that had been forced to leave the country, so by September practically all of our teammates and many other workers had to leave. We, along with two other families from our organization were still there, but the other two families were leaving in two weeks, their visas were expiring as well. We were the only ones who still had valid visas, so we helped those who had to leave.

On August 31, 2006, my husband, my youngest daughter, who was about six years old at the time, and I left in the car on our way to the house of some of our mission companions who had had to leave the country that morning. They could not take all their belongings with them, so we told them not to worry, that we would go and pick up what they could not take with them and keep it at our house for when they could return. We wanted to do everything that day as the next day was Uzbekistan's Independence Day, and usually, the police and army closed the streets and there was always more surveillance. A carload of stuff always attracted more attention, and the situation of so many foreigners leaving did not make us go unnoticed. We didn't want to attract too much attention on the road.

Returning from their house with the things in the car, we were stopped in one of the main avenues of Tashkent. They were men in civilian clothes; we already knew they were not policemen. They looked at the license plate number of our car and immediately looked at some sheets of paper they had in their hands. They had very specific information about us (our full names, address, visa expiration, and which NGO we belonged to. They told us to follow them to a place because they wanted to interrogate us. My husband asked them what the problem was because our documents to be in the country were up to date, but they insisted that we should follow them. At that time cell phone technology was not like it is now, and only my husband had a cell phone. We started to follow the car and soon we realized that behind us there was another car. They had us surrounded, on the road. While my husband was driving, I tried to warn other colleagues to cover us in prayer. We didn't know what was going to happen and we didn't even know where they were taking us.

The car ahead of us pulled into a junkyard (a place for abandoned cars). When we entered the place, we were very nervous. It was a place with old cars, piled up, full of dust, and most of them badly beaten up. The road to enter with the car was narrow so that there was no way to turn around. The car behind us also came in, so we could only go forward. After a few meters, the car in front stopped, and three men got out of it. The car behind us also stopped and three more men got out and stayed behind our car. All these men were from the secret police. We didn't know exactly where we were because it was a place in the city we had never been to before, so we couldn't use our cell phones to let anyone know where we were in case something happened. Very nervous, there in the car with our little daughter we asked the Lord to help us. One of the men with a hand signal asked my husband to get out of the car. My daughter and I stayed inside the car. Sitting down, I could only see my husband talking to these men, and I only prayed for the Lord's protection for him, and for us. Fear wanted to paralyze me, but I prayed to the Lord, and His peace even in the midst of that situation came upon me. I knew that no matter what happened, He was in control. A few minutes later, I saw the gate open, and another car come in. This car belonged to another worker who had also been detained, and just like us, he was escorted by a second vehicle. This worker was one of our teammates who, together with his family, was to leave the country in two weeks. After some time of interrogation, as our colleague showed that he was going to leave the country in two weeks, they were going to let him go, but not us. My husband, realizing that the other worker had permission to leave with his car, asked the police to authorize my daughter and me to go with him. My husband told them that he would stay there with them, and they agreed to let us go. As we were leaving, I prayed to ask the Lord to keep my husband as I did not know if I would see him again. It was definitely a situation that we could not control, and it was totally out of our hands.

Several hours passed and I did not hear from my husband. It was a difficult time, but it was also a time of faith, of believing God that He was in control of everything, that even in the midst of this uncertain situation, Jesus was walking by our side. Through His Word, I found comfort and peace, because I had no way to communicate with my husband. I did not know what was happening. I waited to pray and believe the Lord while my children asked me where their daddy was. After three hours I saw him arrive, without his car. It had been taken away from him. This was the beginning of a time of persecution and harassment for us to leave the country. They came to our house every day to threaten us that we should leave the country.

But the Lord who is good and great did one more miracle. We were able to communicate to our churches the name of the person who had possession of our car. We asked them to pray for the Lord to do a miracle. The police that had taken our car were not the normal police, it was the secret police, KGB type, and these police are above all authority in that place. But God did it, they gave us back our car, two months after they took it from us. The same week before they expelled us from the country, and that same week we managed to sell it." (Abigail)

God sustained this family with His Word, and thanks to the prayers of the many people who intercede for their children in the field. Intercession is powerful, it moves God in favor of his children.

By name His name...

"I was on a trip to the Waraos, indigenous people who live in the Delta Amacuro on the Orinoco River in Venezuela, with a group from a missionary organization from Puerto Rico who were visiting the community for about two weeks. This community is composed of houses made of logs and palm leaves. To walk from one house to another, the indigenous people built a boardwalk. One of the first nights, after worship and returning to the houses to sleep, a girl fell through one of

the boards of the walkway that had broken. They managed to pull the girl out, but she was spurting a lot of blood from her head. The indigenous people, who had heard us talk about a God who heals in the church, instead of taking her to the shaman of the community, brought her to where we were with the permanent missionaries of the community, Peter and Adela. Adela was extremely worried because she knew that it was a way to test us and to test God. The recovery of the girl depended on whether or not they would continue to listen to the Word of God, even if they would leave us in the community to serve.

There were no doctors or nurses among us. I had taken first aid courses and with that, we helped in the health clinics that we sometimes offered. Immediately after they rescued the girl, they brought her to me. She had a wound on her head of approximately two inches or five centimeters. Since it was a head wound, she was leaking a lot of blood, which impressed everyone. I laid her down, shaved the area around the wound, cleaned the wound and put three to four butterfly stitches, and covered her with a lot of antibiotics. Thank God the blood stopped, but the girl was very groggy and that was what worried me, that there was more damage than met the eye. They took the girl home, with some instructions that I gave them, but I immediately indicated to Adela and the group that accompanied me my concern. I told them that we had to pray all night. If the girl spent the night well, everything would be all right. If not, we would be in a lot of trouble. So, we interceded to God that night for the girl.

42

The next morning, the sun reflecting on the waters of the river, seemed to smile. And just as we saw not only the girl smile but also her parents, she was fine. God had heard the prayer, but He had done something else that we did not know. Two days after the girl's fall, I saw a group of children jumping off the dock into the river. They were swimming and playing, laughing a lot. I noticed that among them was the girl. I called her over to check her stitches and her wound, and surprise! The wound was gone. I had to look and look; I could not believe my eyes. There was only the shaved area, but no stitches, no scar, no nothing. Just a small bald spot in the area from shaving, that if it hadn't been there, I would have thought I had been the wrong girl. God had made the miracle visible to them and to us, by His Name and His reputation, God had heard the intercession and had completely healed this little girl. Glory be to God! (Wendy)

God knows our hearts...

God knows the requests of our heart, but above all the intentions of our heart. When we speak to Him with trust, He hears us and gives us not only the peace we need, but the peace that others who claim to believe in Him need to see in us. Obedience to Him and trust in His Word is the best testimony we can give to others of God's care for us. God heard the prayer of a Mexican woman in the field and the answer to that prayer was a testimony to the community...

"When I was 24 years old, I was leaving my country for Mali, a country in northeast Africa, to serve for an indefinite period of time among the Bambara, a Muslim ethnic group. I must confess, I had a fear that only God and I knew. I had heard that Muslim men ended up wrapping up missionary girls to marry them and convert them to Islam. Actually, that made me sad. My fear was that I would end up like one of them, so I constantly talked to God about it and asked Him infinitely to guard my heart and not allow the enemy to deceive me. It was not easy in a culture where marriage is very important. Most activities center around marriages, so the comments constantly came in, friends offering me their own husbands. These moments were opportunities to tell them about Adam and Eve and how God had formed us and there was a man for a woman, etc. But as we got deeper into the friendship the subject always came up. So I talked to God and said, "Please God give me a good answer, something to help me deal with this reality." For now, my answer was "God will give it to me" In this culture parents or some family member can decide who you marry (arranged marriages) so, in a way, they were convinced by this answer. As for me, I was not anxious, I had found fulfillment in Him. I was enjoying my singleness and loving everything that was happening around me. But one day, a very close friend of mine asked me again why I didn't have a man in my life and I replied, "God will give him to me." She stared at me, looked at me fixedly and said, "But you are fighting with God." I felt the blood rush to my feet and my smile went away. I could only say to her, "No."

Being in my room, I talked to God. I let Him know that all the security I had on the subject was gone, lost. I asked God, "Now what do I do if I am not sure, how will I be able to cope with this thing I am going through?"

44

I decided to go on a fasting and prayer retreat. I needed to listen to God urgently. It was urgent to have that closeness that had kept me strong and that in seconds had vanished. I prepared myself and went for three days to a place I found in the city by the Niger River. It was an excellent time. I asked God a question, "I just want to know one thing, am I going to get married? Do you know what he said to me, "Delight yourself in me and I will grant the requests of your heart." So I totally surrendered. I no longer struggled with it and the rest of the time I spent just delighting in His word and His presence. I went back to my routine, talked to my field leaders and they prayed for me. Again, I felt full, in Him taking new strength.

I have to say, God knows the moments. If I had been told before I went on that retreat that, in a couple of weeks, a guy on the other side of the world would be calling me by Skype... I'd have been able to get back to my routine,[11] I would not have believed it (I can draw a smile remembering that moment). But it happens. A Latin guy, who was working in Northwest Asia, who for some reason had been in Mexico, in the same church that had sent me to Africa, was contacting me. (I won't tell in detail how God told us we would get married. I will leave that for another time). We began a long-distance relationship with a view to marriage. What do you think happened when I told my friend that I was getting married? The one who had asked me if I was at odds with God said, "God does listen to you." Truly for all my friends in that land

---

[11] Application that allows international calls through the computer or cell phones.

they were sure that the God I shared with them does listen and cares for his children. (Hawa)[12]

And God came to heal...

Let's go back to Clara, called to missions, serving wounded, and with great pain in her heart. God used her pastor to begin her healing…

"That day I got up and told the Lord what I was feeling that day. I told Him that I was afraid of the pain and of going through what I went through again. That I was afraid of being broken by the pain again. Still, I prayed, believing that despite everything it would be a day when I would not let sadness win. I trusted that strength would be restored in me. I knew that God was walking with me and that He had been my comfort and direction during my twenty-three years of being a Christian. So I went to a meeting with the ministry team of our church and there I began to serve the table with joy not knowing that I had an appointment with the missing key to the door of forgiveness.

At that moment my pastor Luis asked, "Do you know what day it is today?" But no one said anything. He went on and said, "Have you seen Clarita who is joyfully serving the table?" There was silence. And then he said, "Even though it is a difficult day for her because it is the anniversary of her father's death!" I was in shock; it was a trap from the Lord for me. I could not escape from there, but I understood that I was going to do something, so I sat down and continued listening.

---

[12] Pseudonym for security

Pastor Luis asked me, "What are you feeling?" Of course, the tears were not lacking and much less the hidden pain of the chest! So I answered, "Remembering is very painful, because seeing those who did all this causes me pain still in my heart, but I feel I need to forgive!"

The pastor replied, "Yes, it is difficult, especially seeing all that is going on in the midst of a peace process that is not just. Justice requires paying a price and it is not just any price. Jesus paid a very high price. So, forgiveness is not something cheap, it has a very high cost." He went on to tell me on behalf of the LORD, "I am your Father and I love you. You are not alone. I have seen your tears and your pain and with the same comfort that I have comforted you, you will comfort others."

Obviously, the Lord took up his word, to bring forgiveness and comfort, but it was not something for me, but to give to others. "He comforts us in all our sufferings, so that we may also comfort those who suffer, giving them the same comfort that He has given us." (2 Corinthians 1:4)

Of course, I couldn't stop crying because I was understanding what true forgiveness meant. I literally felt waves and waves come over me, waves of His great Love! It was something inexplicable that I had never felt before. And I heard the Lord's voice audibly, "Do you think the only way I can break someone is through pain? NO! I can break through Love too." Yes, it was now more than clear to me. It was true, it was what I was feeling, His brokenness through Love, something that filled me deeply. Now I can say, this is one of God's ways to set us free. Today I can say that I am able to understand and comfort others who have gone through the same thing and that I can look into the eyes of those who hurt me and see them with love. But that is not all. From there God presents us with the challenge of forgiveness. The Word of God, which is very clear, shows us the way.

After thinking, I realized that I no longer felt anger or any adverse feelings. Then the Lord asked me the following question, "What are you doing for those who offended you?"

I replied, "Mmm! Lord! I don't feel anything for them anymore, I don't feel the slightest bit of resentment." - "Then what are you going to do next?":

"You have heard that it was said, 'Love your neighbor and hate your enemy.' But I tell you, love your enemies and pray for those who persecute you, that you may be children of your Father in heaven. He causes his sun to rise on the evil and the good and sends rain on the righteous and the unrighteous. If you love those who love you, what reward will you get? Aren't even the tax collectors doing that?" (Matthew: 5:43-46)"

My response was, "*Yes Lord, I will not resist something that is going to do good for me.*" (Clara)

God walked with me and redeveloped me...but with love

All of us at some point in our lives lament and complain about what we don´t have or why, or simply about what we do not understand. Even the missionaries question many things, but God is so beautiful and loving that every day he extends his mercy and teaches us with love. He redeems us so that we may grow and refocus and look at the things that are not seen, the eternal things.

"In walking each day with the Lord, fears, doubts, unanswered questions, and even fights with God arise. One thing is to go out as a worker alone and another thing is to go out as a family, in both cases, there is much to say and consider. We have a daughter who was twelve years old when we left our country. Today, by the grace and mercy of the Lord, she is already a beautiful woman, beautiful and fearful of the Lord. But surely someone who, like me, went to the countryside as a family, will have heard these words from her children: "I did not ask to be brought", "Nobody asked me if I wanted to come or not". So, I was fighting with the Lord, complaining about something every day. One day I would complain because I could no longer dispose of my money as I used to, another because I had to walk a long way to pick up my daughter from school, and yet another because I didn't see people, I only saw houses and things. I complained because the loneliness intoxicated me or because I could not open the door of my house without being a spy trying to find out where my neighbor's ferocious pit bull was coming from. But it was in the midst of those complaints and fights that one day, on my way, to pick up my daughter, on a warm Floridian noon, and in tears, I recognized that God was walking with me. A movie began to run through my head. It was like watching the people of Israel walking in the desert, some falling, beaten

down by the wind, dust, heat, and exhaustion. I saw it all vividly inside my head. One instant I wondered what this was, while in another instant I felt a strong throbbing in my heart. I could describe it as a small touch, and the clear voice telling me "The people who walked in the wilderness and complained, did not see the promised land." Then it was like a slap on my cheek, and suddenly I understood. I was confronted, for what I was doing. But God, with his great love wiped away my tears, and what flooded inside me was a calmness that I cannot explain." (Mary Fernandez)

God gives us security, even if the earth trembles...

Sometimes we don't understand why we live through certain experiences, but a Salvadoran woman, who had experienced earthquakes in her country, and possibly some other situations that perhaps shook the ground, would experience something stronger. However, God was there to give her security and strength, and to use it to bless Japan....

"Beginning the afternoon of Friday, March 11, 2011, everything changed in the country where I was serving. An earthquake measuring 9.1 on the Richter scale shook the entire country. About 23,000 people died that day. This disaster triggered a second disaster on the northeast coast of Japan, a tsunami of 14-meter waves, which destroyed everything in its path and thousands of people drowned. But the waves were not content with the lives they took, they also generated the third disaster in the area, jumping over the walls of a nuclear power plant in the city of Fukushima, causing seawater to mix

50

with tons of radioactive water and intoxicate the Pacific Ocean.

At the time of the earthquake, I was in a prayer meeting with three Japanese sisters. We did not realize the magnitude of the earthquake and stayed for a couple of hours together sealing tracts of God's word, to go and distribute them another day. However, on the way home I realized the seriousness of the situation, as I saw people in the streets and outside the buildings. The telephone lines were cut and there was chaos in the train system, which stopped running for several days. When I arrived home, there was no one there. I felt a deep loneliness and burst into tears while talking with God and waiting for the arrival of three missionary companions with whom I shared the apartment.

Every day we experienced aftershocks, and because of the anti-seismic constructions of the houses, we felt the movement of the earth in a circular form, giving the sensation of dizziness with the eyes open or closed. These aftershocks were quite frequent day and night. In supermarkets, there were shortages of certain foods. Every day in immigration, thousands of foreigners were requesting a document to leave the country temporarily. My team was aware that God was with us. Those were the best times to share God's love with the Japanese. Every day we met to pray and intercede for the country.

Japanese friends tried to convince me to leave the country for safety reasons for a while. However, God comforted me very much through Joshua 1: 6, 7, and 9; where

God urges young Joshua, again and again, to be strong and courageous and promises to be with him always. Then as I continued reading the whole book, I saw the faithfulness of God fulfilling his promise to Joshua and helped him in every challenge he faced.

God gave me a lot of strength, and then I started praying for the opportunity to travel with my team to the northern part of Japan to help the people affected by the tsunami and nuclear disaster in Fukushima. God answered my prayer. The opportunity came, and my team leaders organized several trips to help the affected Japanese. God gave us strength and so we shared His word in an orphanage. Other weeks we shoveled up all the mud that covered the streets or was inside houses, and then we visited refugee centers to cook and distribute food to 600 people. On one occasion we helped to clear all the mud at a factory where seaweed is processed. The owner of this place was thinking of committing suicide, as he thought it was all over when he saw his factory flooded with mud everywhere, but when he received cleanup support, he felt that he was not alone and that it was worth living. Without God's strength and help, it would not have been possible to support the Japanese. (Carolina Ramirez)

And God kept me…

"Being in one of the North African countries, God allowed me to experience what it means. 'Though I walk through the valley of the shadow of death, I will fear no evil, for you will be with me...'" (Psalm 23: v.4a) I arrived in the country at a very difficult time. Many workers had to leave the country unexpectedly, expelled by the government because of the suspicion that they were Christian workers. Those who remained were frightened by everything that was happening. There was an atmosphere of fear and confusion. This fear affected the workers, but also the national believers. Because of this, many stopped congregating for a while. I wondered how I could share the gospel in the midst of this situation, at a time that did not seem ideal.

On the other hand, the family of workers who had welcomed me assured me that everything would be fine. This family was constantly traveling from one city to another to meet with their team, and I always accompanied them. On one of these occasions, I was returning with another missionary from taking a group of volunteers to a hotel. It was a rainy night and the pavement was wet. Upon entering a highway, the missionary did not notice that there was an overturned truck on the road and its size was blocking both lanes. When she saw it, full of panic she began to shout, "I can't stop it, I can't stop the vehicle." The brakes were not responding and our car was going straight into the truck, there was nothing we could do to stop it. It looked like we were close to death, but to my surprise, I was not afraid. However, in a matter of seconds, two thoughts came to my mind. The first was of my family, especially my mom, and the pain I could cause them if I died a tragic death. The second was the fact that I had just arrived in the country. No one knew me; I had barely shared the gospel, so my death would not be helpful to the advancement of the gospel. I began at that moment to pray and cry out to Jesus for help and suddenly, I heard the voice of the Lord in my mind telling me, "Though you walk through the valley of the shadow of death, you shall fear no evil, for I will be with you." The Lord Himself was assuring me that He was with me and would keep me, that there was nothing to fear. At that very moment the impact came, the blow was to the passenger side where I was. The car was practically destroyed, but miraculously, we were both unharmed. We barely had a few scratches. Even so, we were taken to the hospital, and thanks to God's mercy we had no major injuries, only those caused by the seat belt pressing on our bodies.

The Lord had been with me. Even though I had to go through the trauma of the accident, He was with me to protect me. He never abandons us. He is faithful and true and keeps His promises. He has not promised us that everything will always be all right and that we will never have problems, but He has promised to always be by our side. His protection will be with us. The experience also helped me not to be afraid of the situation the workers were experiencing and taught me to be courageous in sharing the gospel. The experience helped me to share with those who knew that God is close to those who call upon Him and that we can know Him personally. Any fear I might have had for what might happen because of what was happening in the country disappeared and I shared the gospel with courage, trusting that the One who had called me would take care of me." (Amapola de la Peña)

A reconfirmation of its constant presence along the way

"The morning after my mother's death, I had an experience that marked me. I woke up that Sunday, July 19, 2016, very

weak. I came to the living room and did not understand what was happening to me, why was I so weak? I stepped on the carpet where I was prostrating to pray and the inner voice of the Lord inside me said to me, "Take off your sandals, I have to talk to you!" I felt weaker and weaker, and I prostrated myself. I said to the Lord, "I don't understand why I am like this!" But before I finished speaking, He interrupted me and said, "It is I who have taken away your strength so that you may see that the one who gives you the strength you have had was Me." I had put on music to pray and I kept crying and crying. Very weak, I began to feel a deep pain in my chest, a pain that I thought was the same as when one is going to die. I was screaming and crying, what horrible pain! I could not imagine, how could an unconverted person without Christ, go through the pain of the loss of his mother, if I as a believer had such a sharp pain.

I had been in the hospital with my mother and the two women they put next to her passed away. I prayed for the children of these women and after a while, I asked the Lord, "Can I stand up now?" He replied, "I'm not finished yet. Sit down." I was still very weak. He began to bring back to my memory the moment when He called me to serve Him, how He had revealed to me to work for Him, the visions, the dreams, the messages, and miracles He did to confirm to me, again and again, His will. All that went through my mind without leaving a single detail out. Then I said to him, "Yes Lord, yes, I know, I have no doubt that it was you who brought me here!" And he said to me, "I have brought you here so that you can talk about me and teach what I have taught you, I am the one who provides for you and you will never lack anything. I will have them donate to your account and many times, anonymous donations because I want you to know that it is Me and no one else. Do not move from here until I tell you. Some will come to offer you proposals, but they are not mine. You wait for my instructions." I already knew that was the end of the message he was giving me and I asked him, "Now can I get up?" He answered, "Yes. I will give you back your strength little by little, as glass is filled, so I will give My strength back to your body." I confess that never in my life had I had such a consoling experience that so affirmed my faith and empowered me. Little by little I regained my strength up to my knees, by mid-afternoon up to my waist and by evening I had all the strength back in my body. Glory be to the Lord!" (Marta Gonzalez, Spain)

And it is God who inspires us and gives us the strategies and resources to fulfill his mission.

"Then the Lord said to Moses, "See, I have chosen Bezalel son of Uri, the son of Hur, of the tribe of Judah, and I have filled him with the Spirit of God, with wisdom, with understanding, with knowledge and with all kinds of skills..."

Exodus 31:1-3 NVI

"Again and again, God inspires human beings and gives them gifts and abilities so that we can be collaborators in His work and carry the message in every possible way. In many ways, God speaks, and in many ways, man learns; some with music, some with letters, and some with art. Regardless of how the world may understand God's love, He will do His best

to make Himself understood, and use men and women to inspire them to achieve His purpose"

The design of the children's room mural

"Jesus said, "Let the little children come to me, and do not hinder them, for the kingdom of heaven belongs to such as these." Matthew 19:14 NIV

"I had designed the children's room in the church where I attend. Upon seeing it, a sister from another church asked me to design something special for them as well. Their Sunday school room needed a radical change that would motivate the children to want to be there.

I began to pray that God would inspire me. After I knew that the theme of the room was to be Jesus with the children, I proceeded to draw a whole landscape and scene. But then something supernatural happened. As I was painting the children, I began to draw features of different races and nationalities on the children's faces. On several occasions, I felt that someone was directing the brush at me. As I stepped back to see what was painted, I was impressed with the details that were left there. The brethren who were helping witnessed what happened there and we all gave glory to the Lord. When the three-wall mural was finished, about two people were skeptical of the painting and wanted to tarnish the theme of what had been painted. But immediately the Lord inspired me to explain every detail of the painting biblically. I prepared a document with that same explanation, and later I gave it to Pastor Oliver, in case anyone else had any doubts or asked for an explanation of the message of the mural. I can only add that when I myself finished, I was speechless!"

(Marta Gonzalez)

And God used a children's ministry

"One of the groups that God had put on my heart was children. So, that's how I started a ministry for this population in my congregation. I took months to pray to ask God for confirmation, and a team that had the same heart to share God's word with the children. A Japanese sister with whom I met to pray helped me to share the project with the congregation in the Japanese language. My pastors thought it was a good idea so they and their wives also got involved in the project.

We started offering English classes, and at the end of the classes, we told stories of Jesus to the children. My congregation financed the purchase of a program called "Kids Brown," used by Christian schools to teach English, and also purchased the books to be used for four years.

In this ministry God allowed us to develop a friendly relationship with the children and their parents. The children studied hard, in a relaxed and fun way. They enjoyed listening to the stories of Jesus. At the time of the class, only the teachers and the children entered the classroom. However, my friend, Mrs. Yamanaka, now almost 80 years old, was also allowed to attend. She lived alone and loved to be surrounded by the children. She would watch the children's behavior improve over time as they came to our class. We would tell her that it was God's love that changed them. So, God was using the children's ministry to get Mrs. Yamanaka's attention.

Over time my relationship with her allowed us to sow the seed of God's word. For years we prayed for her salvation. We would invite her to the congregation's worship services, although at first, she was not interested. One day she could not resist God's love and received Jesus as her Lord and Savior, just before she passed away. We participated with Mrs. Yamanaka in a variety of activities and our relationship became like that of grandmother and granddaughter. Although I miss her, I know she is now in a better place. God is faithful." (Carolina)

God shows us the way and gives us strategies...

I had been on the mission field for two years. We were working hard to build up the church. But I began to worry about the most vulnerable area of the community. They were very close to us. Five minutes by car, about ten minutes walking. But I had this deep feeling that even in close proximity, we couldn't reach them. To our Children's Church, which was a space created to teach the children of the community about God's love and which we celebrated every Saturday, where many children came. My gaze would stop on them, on the babies. They depended only on their mother or a little brother or sister to take care of them. Many times, they looked extremely thin and sick. I looked at my children, at that time they were four and two years old, and I knew how difficult it was, many times, to be a mother. Especially with no water, no job, and no hope. God was already preparing the soil of my heart, and I began to feel a certain burden for those babies.

One day a woman, a member of our church, came to my door with her dying six-month-old baby. That day I understood the seriousness of the matter. He looked weak and sick. I questioned how, before my eyes, this could have happened. After several days, I learned a little about initiatives that exist in different countries in extreme poverty. For example, how focusing on children at an early age brings many benefits and favorable changes to this population. They taught how to help with cost-effective methods by providing simple things such as oral serum, deworming, and vitamins, things that for many would-be insignificant, but in reality, make the difference between life and death. Together with two young sisters from our church, I started going around the area closest to the municipal dump to see the babies under three years old. We would pray before we left, carry our vitamins, water bottles, oral rehydration solution, and some medicine. There was a lot of need. We started with five children to see if we could see a difference. Some of the children were over a year old and still not walking and had skin diseases and parasites. We hydrated them, gave them vitamins. We saw how they, with so little, reacted positively in an almost miraculous way. They were survivors with purpose. That's how the Ama Nacer project was born. For several weeks we were doing this, and we saw great changes in the children. So, I decided to include more mothers from the community. I visited house to house explaining everything. These apprentice mothers became my mission field.

During the time I was working with these mothers, we offered them various workshops, including a hygiene workshop. We talked to them about early infant development, and they also received workshops on self-esteem, forgiveness, and domestic violence. These workshops were offered by psychologists who soon became part of the project. At every opportunity, the word of the Lord was preached to them, and they were told about the love of Jesus. I knew at all times that my job was to sow the seed of the word, to show the love of God, and to help these children to have the possibility of better health and quality of life. I had never done this kind of work before, but the Lord was putting in my heart every step to take. He is the one who has inspired every detail from the beginning, the name of the project, how to present it, and how to carry it out. God is the one who inspires us, gives us the vision and the strategies. Our Omnipotent God has infinite ideas for visionaries, for those who execute his will. We are limited beings and so are our resources, but we have a God of infinite resources who loves each population and knows what they need. He is a God who is not detached from the culture or the mentality of the one he wants to reach.

In order to be sensitive to the inspiration that God pours on me as a missionary, I must forget about my tastes, needs, styles, and preferences and focus on observing, listening, and learning. My goal should never be to change the lives we impact, but to lead them to an encounter with Jesus

Christ and to the knowledge of how to lead a worthy and pleasing life; fearing God." (Siris, Honduras)

Strategies, strategies, and more strategies...

"The word exhorts us to "pray without ceasing." So, I can tell you that one of the main strategies in a mission is prayer. Jesus spent a lot of time praying, especially before and after he was with the people sharing about the Kingdom of God. Luke 6:12-13 tells us that Jesus "went to the mountain to pray and spent the night praying to God. And when it was daylight, he called his disciples..." Prayer helps us to communicate with God, know His heart, and be directed toward what He wants to do.

Secondly, we must seek the "man or woman of peace" according to Luke 10:6. We believe that God, through His Holy Spirit, is working in people's hearts. We share the gospel, but we expect God to lead us to those whose hearts are already prepared to receive the message. It is important to pray that God will give us the necessary discernment to know with whom we should spend our time. There are people with whom we have shared the gospel many times and in different ways; and they show no interest, so it is important to discern whether we should continue to share with them or move on to allow others to have the opportunity to listen.

Third, Bible stories should be shared and intertwined with the gospel. Faith "...is by hearing and hearing the word of God" (Romans 10:17) so it is important that they hear the word so that it can do what it was sent to do.

Fourth, I would say, is to involve the local church in the mission. The early church was known for "having the favor of the people" (Acts 2:47). Within our team, we have made it our task to involve the local church in our work and also to support those initiatives of the church in favor of the community. We recognize that the local church has the workers and knows the language so they can easily share more the gospel with the unreached who live around them.

As a testimony, I share with you that one of the sisters of the church prayed for about twelve years for the church to start a ministry to reach the unreached in the community. When she shared this with me and another colleague, we set about the task of praying with her and researching what were the needs and interests of the community we wanted to serve, especially the Muslim community. As a result, we started an English class and a literacy class for women. These classes have opened the door to share the gospel with Muslim women. God already has the strategy for each place; we just need to discover it in prayer." (Amapola de la Peña)

God took me to the English classroom

"God led me one morning before 6:00 A.M., to do my devotional at a lake that was about 20 minutes' walk from my house. I took my Bible, my notebook, and my breakfast, and so I started on my way.

When I arrived, I was impressed that there were about seventy elders ready to do exercises together. That day I learned that in different communities the elders meet in parks early in the mornings to do stretching exercises for about twenty minutes. I didn't know anyone, however, as I started the music on a radio they had brought along, I joined in doing the exercises following the movements they were doing. At the end, a Japanese woman in her sixties approached me in a very friendly manner and spoke to me in English. That day she invited me to a group of which she was a member, called "English Salon." That is a Saturday, bi-monthly meeting in which about ten retired seniors participate.

Their level of English is advanced, and they love to learn technical vocabulary and discuss various topics. So, they take articles from a newspaper in English and read paragraphs, and then one by one simultaneously interpret them into the Japanese language. Although my Japanese vocabulary was quite limited, I joined the group. On several occasions, depending on the topic, some people asked me questions and wanted me to answer them from a Christian point of view. It was in this group that I met the elderly woman I came to love as my Japanese grandmother. But we also deepened friendships with several of these elders. Although there are people in the group who consider themselves atheists, they have always given me the opportunity to talk to them about our God. The seed is being sown." (Carolina)

God invited him to my table

"In Colombia, I worked with a large church of about 800 people that had three services on Sundays but was located in a very needy area. I lived very close to the church, which allowed me to see the needs of the community and observe how

they lived. It was a very dangerous area to live in, but the Lord led me there.

I had some neighbors who would go up to the roof to smoke marijuana and the smell would come down to my house, which was on the second floor. It was very uncomfortable for me. One day while I was cleaning the stairs, I prayed to God and asked Him how I could approach them and tell them about His love. At that instant, I heard an inner voice telling me, "Invite them to dinner." So, I did on two occasions. It was beautiful to see how on the second occasion, two of them received Christ as their Savior. What I didn't know was that one of them, Diego, would die two weeks later when his motorcycle was stolen. I did not know that Diego was going to die so soon, but God did and He put in my heart, instruction, and the desire to fulfill it, to invite him to dinner.

As I attended the funeral, I saw his friends' desire for revenge, but being able to be part of the funeral ceremony gave me the opportunity to minister not only at the funeral home but also at the cemetery. This opportunity attracted his friends to attend a memorial service at our church a few days later. So again, I was able to preach to his friends. God allowed the sharing of my table to become a table of blessing, a table of salvation for Diego, a table where Diego passed from death to life." (Maritza Cumba)

Struggles on the road

Although in many places and particularly when it comes to reaching the female population for Christ, being a woman offers an advantage to Latinas in the mission field. It also represents a constant struggle, in the path of women in missions, some with themselves, others with the people around them, and others...well...others...   Here is one of them:

"The Lord rescued me at the age of sixteen and I was blessed to be well discipleship.   I served in Children's Church at the same time I was studying at my church's Bible seminary. After which, I began to disciple young ladies. Moises Mejia, when I heard the command of Matthew 28:19-20, I knew that I wanted to give everything to the God who had given everything for me.   I wanted to take the message of salvation to those to whom no one wants to go, to those people with whom no one wants to be.

At the same time, the man who would become my husband a few years later, God was calling him to go to Muslims in countries where there was no gospel. The Lord gave him the opportunity to go to the country of Albania to help the Handal family, and his heart stayed there. Through the years they kept in touch, and it always remained in him a desire to return, but to stay, not just for a month.

When we got married, and after the birth of our children Keren and David, I was facing many conflicts in my life. The "feminism" movement had entered the country and I could see how women were losing the joy of enjoying their families. They were motivated to seek accolades and positions in society, to gain the world, to gain money and power, even if on the way they lost their family or the opportunity to have one. That was a price I was not willing to pay. But it was a struggle against the current. On the one hand, there was the

Scriptures, giving me the model of the Proverbs 31 woman, and, on the other hand, the world telling me that this was something that infringed on my rights and my personal satisfaction. By January 2017, I was more stable and comfortable in my role as a wife and mother. I had discovered "Revive Our Hearts," a ministry where God, through His special messages for women, was molding me and teaching me how to deal with the ongoing attack against biblical womanhood.

Since God uses all things for our good, everything I learned in this women's ministry has served me well during this time. In some portions of the book, I share how my husband and I have been separated during this time from the coronavirus, which has not been easy. My husband in one country and me alone with my children in another. However, on one of those days when I felt sad about the situation, my husband said to me, "God prepared you for this time with that women's ministry." I believe so, for it has been a time when I have experienced giving my all and even beyond my strength." (Elisabeta Diaz)

Because I am a woman...

"And of the rib which the LORD God took from the man, he made a woman, and brought her to the man."

Genesis 2:22 Reina-Valera 1960 (RVR1960)

Although many women have served in various parts of the world and have established churches, orphanages, hospitals, and others, they often face challenges simply because they are women. There are many positions regarding the subject of women in ministries and work for the Lord, which will not be discussed here; that is another matter. The important thing is to understand that women have been able to deal with this challenge remembering the main thing, that His name is exalted, that more lives be won for Christ and that disciples be formed. Not forgetting that it is for His glory, and not theirs has been essential in handling this challenge. Here are examples of several situations on the subject:

"Being a woman in an evangelical society where not all groups accept women's ministry also posed a challenge. On one occasion when I was a pastor in the church where I was serving in Spain, it was suggested to me not to perform a marriage ceremony because the society was not used to a woman officiating such a ceremony. My performing the ceremony could invalidate the marriage. Since it was not my priority to prove myself to anyone, I agreed." (Ivonne)

"As a particular note, my work in Latin America entailed dealing in a macho world, where only men share and address their peers. However, the cross-cultural and missionary training offered by my beloved Methodist Church in Puerto Rico allowed me to reach out assertively to these leaders. This entailed, at times, lowering my gaze to talk to them, since looking straight ahead was NOT well seen. My behavior, guided by God, allowed me to arrive alone to important meetings, clothed with the Holy Spirit, which allowed me to make significant exchanges. One of these groups was the International Forum of Bible Agencies. I can affirm that His word was fulfilled where it says: "he who

humbles himself will be exalted". - Luke 14:18 (Ana Ibel Santiago)

***

"For me, being in constant prayer with the father has helped me to receive the strategies to be able to minister effectively in a culture where being a woman is more difficult. In my case, I work with Muslim men, this breaks with the norms of Islam. Culturally they do not see it as right for a female to spend time with Muslims. Being connected to the Father and listening to His instructions on how to approach me to fulfill His mission has been key. His grace has led me to them, and God has opened the doors in such a way that I am now part of their family." (Karima)

***

"On one occasion my boss or immediate supervisor could not attend a missionary conference in the United States and asked me to go in his place to make a presentation. It was important to participate because it was an opportunity to offer many Latinos information about the Bible translation ministry and their opportunities to serve. The organizers wrote to my boss, indicating that unfortunately, I could not be their representative because I was a woman, yes, because I was a woman. They clearly stated so. My boss was very upset, as he supports ministries where everyone is equal.

Now, I knew it was important that this ministry be represented, so I made a proposal to my boss. At that time, I had a disciple in the ministry who had already seen me present the ministry several times, so I proposed to my boss to take him with me and have this young man make the presentation. My boss agreed, although a little worried because the young man did not master all the information as I did. But here was the plan; the young man would make the presentation using my ready-made presentation. If anyone in the audience asked any difficult questions, he would say, "Well, that's so simple, my secretary is going to be kind enough to explain it to you." The plan was perfect. Everything went like that, and everybody knew about the ministry. I was not the important one, not even the young man, what was important was the call that those present would receive to collaborate with God's mission." (Wendy)

"As women in the field, I urge you, when you don't know how to solve when your problem is our gender, pray. God will take care of doing what He has to do to draw to you those who need to listen and bear witness that He is with you. That is what happened to me in the middle of a community where, as a woman, I could not speak to the men, in the Orinoco River. I am an agronomist, and as such, I was invited to go to the community of the indigenous Waraos to teach them how they could plant over the water in different ways in their community. The indigenous people there are very hungry because they have no land to plant, so they live by fishing and hunting. When it rains, they cannot fish or hunt, so in times of rain, they go hungry. They travel for two days, to certain places to sow, but when they come back, they don't always find what they have sown, because they steal it. So, the idea was that I would teach them how to sow in small containers that they could keep in their palafitos.[13] I had a lot of seeds with

me.   We called all the men in the community to teach them how to do the planting project at home and to give them seeds, but no one showed up for the class. I saw them all sitting at home as if nothing was happening, doing nothing. I left sad and angry because I was there eager to help and they showed no interest, but they weren't busy either. So, what was going on? In the afternoon, when the missionary in charge arrived, I told him what happened and he said, "Ah, it may be because you are a woman, they are not used to a woman teaching them." What?! and how was I supposed to help them?

Well, that night I prayed about it all and waited. The next day I planted some seedlings in several cups and put them on the edge of a window overlooking the road. And I prayed. Then God appeared.   The next day I noticed some men coming and calling to others and they all came to the window; I didn't know what was going on. I went to the window and surprised, the glasses had plants in them. Miraculously, the seeds that were supposed to germinate in seven days were already plants. I couldn't believe it. God worked a miracle that night. So that day I called all the men back together for the gardening class and what happened?   My class filled up. Not only the men came; but many women and children who wanted to learn. I told them that if they brought containers with a little soil in them, I would give them seeds. That afternoon I saw three men arrive with a canoe full of soil. Since then, they call me "Namutu," the one who sows, even though God made me a woman." (Wendy)

---

[13] This is the name given to their houses built on strong logs over the water.

God opens doors and closes doors...

"Am I now trying to win the approval of human beings, or of God? Or am I trying to please people? If I were still trying to please people, I would not be a servant of Christ."

Galatians 1:10 Reina-Valera 1960 (RVR1960)

"One day my husband said to me as I arrived, "I almost didn't make it home.   On one side of the street, there was a truck changing some electrical wires and on the other, they were pouring cement."   But he managed to take an alternate route and made it to our house.   Sometimes we think that when we have to change direction it is because we are lost, or someone made a mistake.   But there are times when God allows situations that force us to change the original route. We have to make decisions that give the impression that we are disobeying leaders or the authorities we have at that moment, but it is not so. Sometimes it is just a wake-up call from God to remind us that the goal is to be with Him and to try to be in His perfect will.

We believe in respecting the authorities that God places, but as we walk with God, we learn that, if He has subjected us at some point to authority, and there is something that is not working in spite of our attempt to handle some difference, then another path must be taken. If the relationship between members of a ministry is not bringing glory to God, it is time to move. We, humans, are creatures of habit, and change is very difficult for us. God was taking his people to a promised land. They often thought that this was the final goal, but it was not. The goal is to recognize that He dwells in our midst and wants us to dwell in Him as well, obeying Him. Regardless of where you are and what organization you work with, if you are walking with God, the best place to be is with Him and in His perfect will. And Mary confronted a situation that was pushing her onto the right path...

"One thing I learned as I walked in the Lord, was to keep my relationship with Him every day. This was always present in me; it was very much internalized in my mind and in my heart, it was part of my life, it is my life. I stress this because if it had not been so, I would not have been so sure of my calling to the Galicians. In all probability, I would still be in Madrid. The leaders of the missionary organization that sheltered me required me to stay in Madrid for two years to learn the culture and language. However, I did not consider it necessary because I was fluent in Spanish.

God was opening a door for me through Dr. Pablo Rois (r.i.p.), who was a Doctor of Medicine and Psychology, and Pastor of the Good News Church in Pontevedra, Galicia. He was inviting me to work with him in various ministries in the church. It was what I had been praying for all that time since I arrived in Madrid. I felt that God was answering my prayers and that "that" was the moment. But when I shared with the Agency leaders in Madrid what I saw as a move of God in my life and an answer to my prayer, they didn't understand it that way.

Trying to communicate my feelings in another language to my leaders, in this case, English, was not easy. Something always escapes you or you don't say everything you really want to say. We had several meetings and disagreements, to the point that I had to resign from the Agency. So, I left for Galicia, with the unconditional support of my sending church in Puerto Rico, which I have always counted on, and that of my pastor at the time, Inés Jiménez de Figueroa. Both she and my church supported me at all times. In the end, I was able to go to Pontevedra, Galicia, to work with Dr. Pablo Rois Dios (r.i.p.). There I fulfilled the four years of the economic commitment that my church-missionary-agency[14] to do with me and the mission. All the tasks entrusted to me were fulfilled; everything was recorded in the report presented to the church. It was beautiful to see in those years how the young people of the church were united, how people were converted to the Gospel, and after exactly four years of the Agreement, I returned to my Island.

Many years later, I kept reflecting on this issue of interpersonal relationships in the field and how I had to make the decisions I did. I keep asking myself if I did it right or not, who do you obey first, your leaders or the voice of God? My leaders' intentions and advice were good advice and well-intentioned. There is a hierarchy that must be obeyed. This is so because it is very true that if you do not obey your leader whom you see, how do you say you obey God whom you do not see? There are many questions that I still ask myself despite the time that has passed. For example, what would have

---

[14] The missionary thus refers to the church to which she belonged in her country of origin, which had a missionary vision and which, by sending and supporting her, became her sending agency to the field.

happened if I had listened to my leaders and not to God's voice that "that " was the time to leave for Galicia? And I answered myself: "Maybe Loly (Galician woman and alcoholic) would not have accepted Jesus before she died. Maybe Jorge (homeless, alcoholic, Galician) would not have been baptized and continued in rehabilitation. Perhaps the young people (almost all with talents for music and worship) would not have had the opportunity to work together and some of them accept their call to be pastors or worshipers or leaders... as later happened. Or maybe they did? Or maybe it would be at another time?" There are no concrete answers. What I did learn is that "the harvest is ready" ... and that we must insist in season and out of season.

Getting to know and accept each other in the field team takes a long time. Only one thing I know, it was clear to me that God was calling me to Galicia and that this was the door He was opening. For how long? I still keep the letter invitation to return to Pontevedra that Pastor Pablo Rois (r.i.p.) gave me in 2004 at the end of my time-commitment for four years: missionary-church-agency. It is a pity that he died not long ago, and we could not make this invitation to return to work with him. God continues to be faithful, and His Word and time have shown me that "that" was His precise time for me to fulfill the task that He had in store for me. And now I am on another mission, from Him. (Maria Toro)

"From thirteen to fourteen years I worked with an organization to which I was sent by the missionary organization to which I belonged. There I occupied various roles and we were like a family. After a change in leadership,

the environment also began to change. The family began to fall apart, my new immediate supervisor demanded an explanation of my slightest decision and/or move. He took away responsibilities, team members, and finally, changed my position without telling me. I found out about my new role from a person from another partner organization in a hallway in the middle of an event. I could not believe what was happening. I felt humiliated, sad, and disappointed. A myriad of feelings washed over me. I didn't understand why I was being treated this way. I didn't understand his attitude towards me, even though I asked him several times, because I knew that this person was not evil.

But God was with me, and He was not silent. He used a sister to speak to me. She said to me, "You are leaving it up to someone else to decide what you are going to do for God." Those words, which I knew were from God, calmed my crying. Recognizing that God had placed that person in that position, I knew something was going on; either God was working with something in my character, or it was time to change ministries. I decided to take a time of several months for prayer and seeking God's direction. My time off completed, the same day I returned, and still not knowing exactly what God wanted, I opened my computer to read the emails and begin to catch up on everything that had happened during my absence. As soon as I did that I began to cry in anguish. The pain and sadness were so great that I closed the computer and fell to my knees on the floor. I was saying to the Lord, "You have to talk to me, what's wrong? What is your will? What do you want me to do?" Immediately God gave me a name, and said, "Call her."

It was the person who had recruited me for that ministry. It had been many years since I had spoken to her, but I kept hearing God's voice telling me, "Call her."

Obediently, I called my friend, not knowing if that was still her phone number. It turned out that it was. She was surprised but glad of my call. I told her everything that was going on, crying while speaking and then she said, "Do you remember that I came out of that ministry the same way? It was your husband who gave me a word to confirm that I had to go out and change, and just today I wrote a newsletter sharing that testimony. I'm going to send it to you, but you already know the answer. Verbalize it." I said, "I think so, I already know the answer." As soon as I ended the call, I read his bulletin and went back to the floor. "Sir, it's time to change ministries, it's time to go back to the organization that sent me and it's now. I understand and I will do it." At that very moment, I experienced a miracle. I felt like a hand entered my chest and took away the anguish and pain and gave me peace and joy. I immediately stopped crying and began to laugh. I was filled with joy and began to praise Him for a long time. Needless to say, God already had worked for me in the organization to which I returned, and the work of my hands there has prospered. There is a time for everything, it is time to change. Both organizations are God's, but my time in one was over." (Wendy)

Stones or bridges

We humans often tend to dismiss ourselves when we know God's plans or when we believe He is calling us to something great. Moses said he couldn't speak, Jeremiah said he was a child, Sarah and Zechariah's wife felt old for what God had for them. But God fulfills his purpose in spite of everything, time, money, and even us. That has been the case with some sister missionaries, who saw stones where God wanted them to see bridges.

"A woman, a nurse by profession and already in her second pregnancy, went to the Regional Hospital in her area. That doctor on duty told her over and over again "that is for tomorrow ma'am, besides I have no beds available." The woman returned home, and as soon as she was placed in bed, her baby was born. The child was not breathing, and her color was blackish-.... immediately after her mother was bleeding to death. The woman's mother, who had received the Lord months before, knew that both her granddaughter and her daughter were in danger. She got down on her knees to cry out to the Lord. After a few minutes, she testified, a piercing light illuminated that room. The baby breathed and began to cry, and the mother's bleeding stopped. That woman, who almost lost her life in childbirth, was my mother, and that child, who was stillborn, was me. The Lord paid a special visit that day. God put a particular breath, a breath of life in me after they did not want to take care of my mother in the hospital. Of the three children my mother had, I was the healthiest. I never set foot in a hospital---only for my tonsils, and that was when I was eighteen.

My primary schooling was with missionaries in a North American school, where I learned and mastered the English language from the preschool level. Those missionaries took great care to form my character and my way of being. It was part of the plan that God had for me. Although I felt the call to the missionary field since I was eighteen years old, this call materialized much later. I worked tirelessly in different churches with young people, with worship and music, and as part of their leadership. I had the opportunity to complete a master's degree in Public Affairs and Human Resources at the University of Puerto Rico (UPR). In addition, the Lord awarded me with a scholarship to attend the course for state and local government executives at the John F Kennedy School of Government at Harvard University. I administered for sixteen years a research and training center for the high level of the Government of Puerto Rico, attached to the Office of the President of the UPR.

Everything, but absolutely everything that was said before was...undoubtedly a preparation from my Lord to use it in that particular missionary work that He had for me as part of His plan. In a missionary congress, I met one of the main ministries in the world dedicated to Bible translation. After sending my membership application, an invitation arrived, with expenses paid to the orientation course. The director of that course, after seeing my C.V., asked me to attend the course.[15] *invited me to do an internship in international relations at the sister organization of the NGO I met, dedicated to the development of indigenous people and their mother tongues, in addition to Bible translation. At the end of that internship,*

---

[15]C.V. stands for curriculum vitae, the set of studies, positions and/or work experience that a person has obtained throughout his or her life.

God confirmed that I would serve Him in this area since He had prepared me for it from day one.

It was that academic and work preparation, in addition to His call, that provided me with the tools so that at the age of fifty-two I began to work as a Government Relations Officer for that NGO, both at the local level in Oaxaca, Mexico, at the national level in Mexico City, as well as in two of the entities that deal with indigenous issues at the United Nations. My task is to advocate for, create relationships and agreements in favor of native language speakers and their development. We facilitate training programs from literacy to university level, prepare dictionaries, grammars in mother tongues, as well as technical applications. These tasks are the preamble required to translate the Scriptures.

All our work is framed in a faithful and true testimony of God's love in our hearts, just as He loved me since He formed me in my mother's womb." (Ana Ibel Santiago)

God will supply according to His riches in glory....

"The silver is mine, and the gold is mine," declares the Lord Almighty."

Haggai 2:8 New International Version (NIV)

One of the areas that God works strongly in all those whom He calls is that of finances. Women called to the field are no exception. The fear of not having the money that we need or believe we need to sustain ourselves in the field is one of the weapons that the enemy tries to use to stop the walk of God's daughters. But it is in the finances where the missionaries see great miracles. They are the first to be blessed when they obey and respond to the call when they trust and depend completely on Him. God is not only the owner of gold and silver, but He uses whomever He has to use to bless His daughters in the field, even people who do not know Him. He does it only out of love for his daughters and in fulfillment of his promises. And since God is also Creator, He manifests His creativity not only in letting us know that He will supply, but He uses many ways to do it. Some missionaries share with us their experiences in this area.

They are coins for me

"One of the great concerns of almost every human being is "money." With it, we survive on this planet. Everything is buying and selling, supplies, bills, rents. Even though we Christians want to deny it over and over again, this issue of "economic resources" many times makes us lose focus of the most important thing, which is "faith". I am not a woman with my feet in the clouds, as many might think. I have lived long enough on this earth to know that, if I don't have cash, there are benefits that I will not be able to obtain.

Some time ago I had asked God for a job with a schedule that would allow me to raise my children and spend more time with them, a job where the pay would be enough to live on and where I could give a living wage to the caregiver. God granted me a public job, with all these conditions that I had asked for before. It was a job with a schedule that allowed me to be the one to raise my children, taking care of taking them to and picking them up from school, preparing their meals, and spending time with them. This job not only gave me personal satisfaction, but it was also a job with which I could support my family. It was the first time in my life that I had a decent salary and a position in which I felt comfortable with the possibility of moving up the ladder... "The kid's dream!"

As time passed, I received an invitation to enter the Transcultural Training Institute in Cordoba (CCMT), where I was interested in studying. Unfortunately, I had no money saved; I was coming out of bills I had generated before I got my job. I always kept some cash for the unexpected, but it was not enough to "cross the pond," much less to cover the next six months of training.

Although I hoped that God would open doors in the financial area to support us in this preparation, my reason was against my hope, and I did not understand how this would be possible. After all, who was I? No one knew me, no one knew about me or my calling, although an email was already circulating among my contacts and friends. There was also a video on the networks that a friend had kindly prepared for us, but who was I that someone would invest in me?

At times, I would say to myself "God will provide, He will." Yes, He is opening these doors, therefore, that money must also come...but doubts are also part of the process, doubts that bother God. I think in some ways He just expects us to believe without doubting. Sometimes I imagined Him saying

"Hey, I am GOD the one who opened the Red Sea, the one who created the universe. Should I remind you of my power?"

Two months after our departure, there were some donor pledges, we also had the cash for a ticket, and shortly I was to sign off on my job. One afternoon like so many others, after dropping the kids off at school, I went for a walk. As I was walking on a small track in my city park, these thoughts began to sink in like thorns in my mind. "What will I do, what if we don't make the sum, Lord, what if I made a mistake? Sir, no one knows me, who will support a woman alone with three boys? These doubts, like poison, began to slowly creep into my head.

I began to pray: "Lord, I believe in you, I believe in you, I believe in you, I believe in you! I began to repeat it over and over and over again. I began to hear, "Deborah, run, don't stop!" As an almost unconscious act, my feet began to pick up the pace, I was circling the track and He was saying, "Don't hesitate, just keep running. Haven't I shown you? Don't hesitate, don't be afraid." As I was running, I couldn't stop crying, it was a mixture of gratitude and faith welling up inside me. At one point I said, "Lord, it's a lot of money..." He replied, "Deborah, it's coins for me!" By then I looked at my watch. I had been jogging for more than half an hour my legs began to burn, but I was not tired. It was a special time where I worshipped God within me. He kept repeating to me, "Keep running, don't hesitate, they are coins for me." There were some people on the track, and I wanted to stop for a moment because now I was really tired. But He didn't let it end like that and He told me very clearly: "Stop, raise your hands and worship" ... Well, at that moment I said, "Lord, the park is full, they're going to think I'm crazy."   "Raise your hands and worship." I went around one more time and I was trying to tell myself, "I can't be disobedient." Amazing, isn't it? The Living God speaking, guaranteeing His providence, and all He was asking in return was my worship.   While I, a woman who was living the most beautiful thing in the world, was ashamed that they thought I was crazy.   But at last, I stopped and with my hands raised to heaven, my knees on the ground, and with tears in my eyes, no longer caring about anything else in that sublime moment, I worshipped my Lord!

After running for more than thirty minutes, which is no small thing for someone who only walks, I did one more lap, now breathing softly to catch my breath, meditating on the privilege of having heard his voice, over and over again repeating: "They are coins for me".   There was no one on the track anymore (I think I scared them away!).   I concluded my lap at that place where I worshipped God and for some reason, I turned my eyes to the ground and lo and behold, shining on the pavement was a one Uruguayan peso coin.

I picked it up and smiled ... Lord, they really are coins for you." (Deborah Pampillon, Uruguay)

God gave me a place to live and to minister

"In my ninth year of service in Japan, God put it on my heart to move to serve Him in another Youth base with a Mission (YWAM), whose common language was only Japanese, in order to become fluent in that language and to reach deeper into the hearts of the Japanese.

This change meant renting my own place to live. Without having the resources to do so, I walked in faith toward what God had directed me to do. With difficulty paying, I rented a shared apartment with three non-Christian Japanese women. Each had a mini room in which we could only fit a bed and a small table. I lived there for three months. Although I suffered in different ways in that place, God allowed me to share His love with my three Japanese roommates.

But my Heavenly Daddy had a surprise for me. He miraculously provided a two-story, Japanese-style house for me to live alone for the first time. In Japan, to rent an apartment or house you have to go through a process through a real estate agency, have a good income, and make about five payments before moving in.

God worked a miracle, as I did not have to go through the real estate agency because the mother of the owner of the house is very fond of the ministry I serve. It is very rare in Japan to go through a process like the one I went through. I was able to do the whole process of renting the house directly with the owner, without intermediaries, without making the five advance payments before receiving the key to the house, without a co-debtor, and with a one-page contract, which was not strict at all.

When I came to live in the house, it was empty, with only a kitchen. In Japan, you have to pay to throw away large items. So, I said to God, "Father, please bring into the house only what you know I will need." The first month I ate on the floor, and so I welcomed three Latinos into the house. Just when we were about to develop a meeting with my team to invite Japanese people and talk to them about the meaning of Holy Week, God equipped the house with twelve new chairs and two new tables. This was the first of many meetings I held to talk about God to the Japanese. The times when I did the numbers and saw that I would not be able to pay the rent, I felt that it would be my last month living in the house. But God confirms that I will continue to live there. He has sent me large items that I have needed; so one day a family refrigerator arrived, and another day a washing machine, both in good condition.

I have dedicated this house to hold meetings sharing the word of God, receiving Latinos who come to Japan, and hosting them. Also, I call it "my mountain of prayer." The house looks like a restaurant, some Japanese say. It has the basics, but I am happy using it for divine purposes. Glory to God!" (Carolina)

Jehovah Jireh, announces his blessing by telephone

"Knowing God as Jehovah Jireh, God the provider has been a great experience for me. Personally, I like to share everything I have. I was raised in a home where my mother, from the little we had, shared with the neighbors, who were poorer than us. Knowing that God not only provides for my needs but gives more to help many, has been one of the great experiences of my walk with God. I remember once while serving in Cali, I received a call from a person who had begun to visit my church in Puerto Rico, and he told me: "You don't know me. I have been visiting your church for six months and I

want to send you six hundred dollars for your missionary project in the jungle." That was just the amount we needed to finish the Missionary House we were building on the Pacific Coast of Colombia. On another occasion in Bogota, I received another call from someone asking: "How do I get three thousand dollars for you? One thousand dollars for you and two thousand dollars for your projects. With this call, God was fulfilling a word he had already given me. He had told me that He was going to surprise me with how and where the resources would come from. He is my sustenance, and my provision comes from Him. Such is God, Jehovah Jireh." (Maritza Cumba)

God paid for my vacation

"During Holy Week 2019, I traveled to the Canary Islands to evangelize the children there and to offer some training workshops to teachers of children. Everything went very well; in fact, it exceeded my expectations. But on my departure from the island, I mistook the time of my return flight. There was no later flight until a week later. I would have to buy another ticket. For a moment I was troubled, but I prayed and asked the Lord to work on my behalf even though it was my mistake. And He answered. Friends and family began to send me donations, so many that I was able to buy the other ticket, pay for lodging, and take a week's vacation with expenses paid by my Father. In fact, I was even able to enjoy a wedding that made me feel the Lord's company in this place in a very special way." (Marta, Spain)

Miracles in provision are one of God's specialties. There are so many testimonies of how God supplies, that I think a book should be written just for that. But God not only supplies at the moment of need but even before we know there will be a need. That's what this testimony is about, how He supplied even before we knew what was going to be needed.

"By God's direction, I organized a group of young people from my church to take them on their first missionary experience. After we prayed for a while, God told us the destination, we would go to Haiti. A friend of mine works there as a full-time missionary, and when I discussed the idea with her, she was fine with it. So, I set to work in the preparation of the youth and adults who would accompany me. We spent a year preparing and praying for it.

That day we agreed to meet at the church and from there we would leave for the airport in a bus that a brother from the church had. We were a group of sixteen people. We were ready to leave when a brother arrived with an envelope. He said, "Sister, I didn't have much to give, but I put together these three hundred and twenty dollars from everything I found at home for you to use for whatever you need." I thanked her and we left. We traveled from Puerto Rico to the Dominican Republic by plane and from there by bus to the Haitian border. We would sleep in Pedernales, the border town with Anse Pitrés, Haiti. The morning we were to start work in Haiti we went to the border and were immediately stopped in Haiti, by a very tall woman with a "very unfriendly face." She insisted that we had to pay to enter Haiti. The missionary friend of mine asked her why because in Haiti, there was no entry tax, that she passed through every day and had knowledge of the requirements to enter the country. My friend insisted on asking her to allow us to pass because we were going to serve her country. But the woman said no. We asked her if it was a payment every day and she said, "No, it is a one-time payment." Suddenly and very rudely she shouted at us, "You have to pay twenty dollars per person, if you don't pay, you don't get in! Only you, who live around here, don't have to pay!" He turned his back on us and walked back into the office from which he had come out. My friend was very upset, but I immediately did my math, twenty dollars for sixteen people, what do you think, three hundred and twenty dollars! God had given us the entrance money before we knew we had to pay! The enemy was not going to stop us at the entrance! I told my friend, "God is going to pay." So, we went into the office, asked for a receipt for everything, and went to serve." (Wendy)

Our source is God, it is from his hand that we receive everything.

"When we have a situation, we always tend to seek the solution as humans. Time and time again, God has to remind us that it is to Him that we must first turn. So, when I think of God's people who one day complained that they had no food or water, forgetting the mighty miracles they had already experienced, I don't judge them. I believe that in the end, we are all the same. We forget and complain again, or we simply try to solve it on our own. That happened to me one day. Even though I had seen God come to my house so many times, God came back to teach me a lesson. He wanted to let me know

clearly that when He wants us to do something, He will supply what is needed. Our sustenance comes from Jehovah.

In 2010, the Third Lausanne Congress of World Evangelism was being held in Cape Town, an event that would bring together 198 countries and where many topics of utmost importance for the times to come would be discussed. To participate in this event, you had to be invited, and I was blessed to be one of those invited to attend. I was selected to participate because I was a Puerto Rican woman, and as a representative of Wycliffe in the topics of Bible translation. This event would take me ten days between the trip and the days of the event. It entailed many expenses: lodging for ten days (eight hundred dollars, since it was a very expensive city), the participation fee that included food (eight hundred dollars more, established by the organizers), and the ticket to Africa (one thousand three hundred dollars). In order to participate, I had to miss almost two weeks of my secular work, so I had to stop earning my salary for those days since it would be an absence for personal reasons. In spite of all this, I was sure that God wanted me to be there.

I have been in the same church for many years and have always worked in missions there, so I asked for help with some of the expenses. Since my church is very missionary, I had the idea that they would surely give me a large offering, without knowing how the board made financial decisions, nor knowing the financial responsibilities of the church at the time.[16]

---

[16] Quiero aclarar que mi iglesia siempre me ha apoyado en todo lo que hago, lo ocurrido estaba bajo el control de Dios para darme una lección.

Three weeks before the event, I inquired about the church's response and was told that they were going to give me an offering of two hundred dollars. I felt like I was hit with a bucket of cold water. It gave me a feeling of sadness and abandonment, which I could not understand. It was not the fact of the money that gave me pain, it was the impression I got of abandonment, of orphanhood. I saw it as an offering for anything or anyone. I had never asked for money for anything and when I did, I was offered something that I could not afford. I immediately went to the altar to cry inconsolably and tell God how I felt. I asked Him if He really wanted me to go to that event. I expressed that I was willing to go, but I didn't know what to do, I had no money for any of the expenses. But God did not wait. A sister knelt down beside me, hugged me, and God told me through her, "Don't cry, I invited you and I'm paying." She stood up and returned to her seat. You can imagine how I looked; my eyes almost popped out in shock. That sister didn't know anything. I instantly stopped crying, wiped my tears, and sat down to worship with my brothers.

The next day my miracle began. My immediate supervisor at the ministry calls me and says, "Wendy, I was invited to the Lausanne event, and I cannot attend. I am going to send you my ticket money so you can buy a ticket to represent me there. I immediately thought: "well, I already have a ticket, but I still need lodging, registration fee and food". Two days later, I received an email from one of the organizers of the event, telling me that I had been selected as a facilitator of one of the discussion tables, so they were going to give me a scholarship, which would be equivalent to the cost of the registration fee with meals included. What! I could not believe it, I had not applied to be a facilitator, nor did I know how I had been chosen. I remember running like crazy with my laptop to my husband to show him the email, I could hardly believe it. Airfare, registration, and meals; God had already supplied two thousand one hundred dollars, He was paying.

The following Sunday, I arrived at the church with some prayer letters, indicating to my intercessors that I needed prayer for the money I needed for the trip, that is, the lodging, and for God to help me to see how I was going to balance my paycheck since I would stop receiving approximately one thousand dollars because of my absences from work. A man who was visiting the church, whom I had never seen before, asked me what I was distributing. I explained and he told me to give him one of those letters. I replied, "Of course," and handed it to him. Before he left, he asked me how much I was giving up going on that trip, to which I replied, "One thousand dollars." He gave me a sign with his hand that he understood and left.

Tuesday night at the church prayer service the man returned to the church. Before he left, he handed me an envelope and said, "A small offering for your trip." I thanked him and threw the envelope in my wallet. But when I got home and opened it, I almost fainted. There was a check for two thousand dollars with a note that read, "Eight hundred for your lodging, the thousand you stop earning and the rest for any emergencies." I never saw this man again; God sent an angel to complete the payments for the entire trip. Even for the emergency that actually happened upon my return. I experienced another adventure where I had to make use of the extra two hundred dollars." (Wendy)

Called by God... What?!

All, absolutely all Christians are called to serve God, but not all in the same way or to the same extent. We all have the ability to hear God's call and the opportunity to choose to respond or not to this call. Many times, we have heard the question, how did God call you to missions? It is a genuine question, particularly for those in particular who are already feeling the call in some way or another. Will I be one of those people? The truth is that God does not call everyone equally. The audible voice of God will not always be heard, it is not usual to see angels or some heavenly messenger. God knows how to call his sons and daughters to the task. Here you will find some of the different ways God called some of the women who have shared their experiences in this book.

Hear to obey

"Although I had not yet met Jesus, my first experience with Him was when I was twenty-six years old. I was undergoing surgery when, all of a sudden, I felt myself plunging very deep. I saw myself in a roller coaster-like car at an unimaginable speed. I saw a tunnel where I was going, and everything was dark. I was dying!

Suddenly I saw a giant hand and the splendor of a light. The car began to rise following the glow. A drain cover opened, and I stepped out into the street where the hospital was located. Minutes later I was waking up!

Three long years passed, and it was on November 29, 1988, when I came to know Jesus as my only Savior. Until now I continue on this walk. I can say that Jesus manifested Himself with power in my life from day one and even before I met Him. Two days after I accepted Jesus, He Himself appeared to me at the foot of my bed in a vision. He was so real! His robe was white and crossed by a light blue color. His hair was light brown and wavy and I saw Him with His hands stretched out towards my bed when I heard Him in an audible voice say to me, "Marcela, you are going abroad!" That was how my walk with Him began.

I am a person who is passionate about God. He, who is so wise, knew how to manifest Himself in my life and led me to want more of Him. I always went to the front of the room at congresses and services to receive a word that would encourage me in my calling and confirm it. That same year, in a congress, a pastor called me and I received the following word from God: "You have a great ministry. You will travel to many places. I see a hand of fire in your hand. God will raise you up!"

Hearing to obey is an unusual phrase. We can all hear words and stand there, paralyzed, afraid and with no attitude to follow through. But we can also obey and come out of our comfort. When God reveals a word to us it is not immediately that it will happen. There are processes of teaching, preparation, renunciation, obedience and a price to pay.

The great servants of God from the Old Testament went through all that process as first happened with Abraham who answered the call when he was seventy-five years old. With Joseph there was no difference. He was seventeen years old when God showed him in a dream what would happen in the future. He was sold by his brothers as a slave and came to Egypt. It was twenty years or so until the next meeting with his family by which time Joseph was second only to Pharaoh.

Like Abraham, Joseph, and other servants, I too had my process. From a small one to a bigger one. The grace of the Lord has always been present and we are the ones who allow it to manifest in our lives by accepting the corrections, the treatment, the renunciations, and the calling, but above all to recognize who we are in God. God's grace is infinite, and it is by it that we can walk in the fields to which God leads us. It has been by that same grace that God has allowed me to travel; to teach, disciple and train ethnic community leaders in programs for the development of literacy materials in Peru. That same grace took me to Paraguay and later to live in Brazil. All because of his grace." (Jenny Marcela Cuadros)

***

"Would you be willing to go to my country, China, and tell my people that God is real and that He loves us?"

""Through the preaching of a pastor from Brazil named Edison Queiroz in 1990, God spoke to my heart. He showed me that, in the same way that I had not heard the gospel, there were many people in the world who had not heard the gospel even once, that they were on their way to eternal death because they were trying to save themselves by their own merits.

At that very moment, I thought about the fact that most missionaries continued to go to the same places where the gospel had already been preached. They did not go where Christ had not been named. I remembered, "How then shall they call on him in whom they have not believed? and how shall they believe in him of whom they have not heard? and how shall they hear without a preacher? and how shall they preach unless they are sent?" (Romans 10:14, 15a) That day God specifically called me to "strive to preach the gospel, not where Christ had already been named, lest I build on another man's foundation..." (Romans 15:22) Although I did not consider myself a very courageous person, but in response to his call, I prayed to the Lord saying, "Lord, I want to go where the gospel has not been named, where no one wants to go. You know where I can go."

In 1995 God gave me a "Macedonian" call in my work. God speaks to us at all times and through whom we least expect. I was providing training to a person who had come for a few months from one of our affiliated companies in China. At the end, he asked me about what I did in my free time. I shared with him about my travels to different countries to share the good news of salvation and God's love. Immediately this man asked me, "Would you be willing to go to my country, China, and tell my people that God is real and that He loves us? I have seen many people in churches when I travel, but I didn't know why." At that time, I replied that maybe someday I could go, but inside my heart, even though I had prayed to go where the gospel had not been named, I thought China was too far away. So, I committed to pray that someone might go. Sound familiar? God miraculously opened the door and the following year I traveled to China for two weeks. I went to distribute Bibles both in Hong Kong and other places in China. I evangelized and prayed in Hong Kong. I also had the privilege of meeting a brother in Beijing who was imprisoned for over 20 years for being a Christian.

Even though God manifested Himself in the trip in a special way, I felt a lot of fear there, I cannot deny it. China is a communist country where the Word of God cannot be shared openly. I thought about my human capabilities, my own strength, and how they would not allow me to return to such a place. But as Isaiah 55:8 says "for my thoughts are not your thoughts, neither are your ways my ways..." God kept in my heart the desire to return to China. Although I traveled to other places in Central and South America, Europe and North Africa, China would not leave my heart. So, I could no longer resist God's call. I left my family, my church and my profession in a respectable workplace, and went to China as a missionary, under the cover of my Baptist church and an American missionary organization." (Amapola de la Peña)

Waiting of the world...

"My name is Gabriela, and I am Mexican. My love for missions was born in my childhood. I grew up watching movies about missionaries, such as William Carey, missionary in India; Hudson Taylor missionary in China, and the movie called "The Waiting of the World". These movies impacted my life even as a child. They caused me to grow in me the desire to be a missionary. I didn't know how that could be, but I prayed to God to make it possible at some point.

My family is pure pastors; uncles, cousins and even my parents, but no missionary, so it would be difficult for my dad to let me be a missionary. It was an unknown and taboo subject for him and the church. Both my dad and my church had the idea that missionaries suffered, were killed, starved or simply that it was a very difficult job. Therefore, the church, or at least the church in Mexico, is not as involved in missions as it should be. So I resigned myself to working in the church and there I took on a number of roles, but none of them were fulfilling. I felt that I could do something more to share God's love with people in places where it was not as accessible and where the Word of God was not reaching.

Sometime later, a group of missionaries came to the church where I was, to collaborate with evangelism, and it was with them that I had the opportunity to do what I desired so much. I talked to my father and insisted. I told him that I felt that God was calling me to serve him in this way.

For many years his answer to my concern was no, but at my insistence he confessed to me that he did not want me to leave at that time, because just at that time his business was going bankrupt. He said that he was not going to have money to support me, for travel expenses and everything that was necessary, since we knew that, in that organization, each one had to bear his own expenses. I insisted and told him that God was going to supply my needs (at least that's what I remembered from the movies I saw of missionaries, and I had heard testimonies of what God could do). So, in the end he agreed. I went to this missionary organization where I worked for eight years, and God was faithful to supply me.

Working with children in indigenous communities in southern Mexico, I have seen their needs. Despite the language difference, we teach them to do arts and crafts, games, and plays, all with a focus on the Word of God. We have seen God's hand many times in supplying us with all the materials for the Summer Bible Schools, also to feed them. We have seen the response in the children, we have seen that the Word has made changes in their lives in an integral way. I am a missionary, and I will continue to be one, I love doing missions." (Gabriela Castro)

Go and do...

"I prayed for missions, but I was not willing to leave my position, let alone my comfort zone. But in 2000, during a prayer meeting, I was confronted to leave everything. And what was everything to me? A job with a Master Technician position in Ultrasound, something I was passionate about; a church that was a model for many others; a group of twelve couples that I discipled with my husband; the meetings with the young women and so much more. In addition, I could not think

of having my family far away. I come from a large family, we are currently eight siblings, plus nieces and nephews and great-nieces and nephews. We were always a very close-knit family and one that celebrated life's important events, so this would be very difficult. It was a four-to-five-year process between preparation and departure.

I, the one who prayed for the nations that still do not know about the Lord; the one who investigated fields to know how to pray with understanding; the one who raised a flag of a country as adoption (without knowing much yet); the one who every Saturday prayed because workers are needed in the fields, ended up being confronted and called to respond to the command: GO and DO." (Mary Fernandez)

A wide road of green pastures...

"God called me to missions shortly after I accepted Jesus as my Savior and it began to change my life. In the middle of a dream, I was walking down a wide road of green pastures and coming to a community with children which I introduced to visitors. It was not a normal dream, for to this day I have never had another one like it. From that night on, I was certain that one day I would be in another land. I always asked the Lord: When will this be? But there was no answer. Two years passed, and I met the man who is now my husband. Soon after, we were married. His parents are pastors of a church in Puerto Rico, the Church of 1st Corinthians 13. Pastors Pedro Montañez Serrano and Maria Elena Aviles at that time were making missionary trips to Honduras, already for fourteen years. There they had built a temple that they used

in the summertime to offer food, medicine, and clothing, among other things. The Pastor had been trying for some time to find someone to pastor that congregation. After two years and after being part of one of these trips, I told my husband that we could be the answer to the need for pastors there.   To my surprise, he had been very quiet about his missionary calling for years. So when I told him this, we agreed to present the idea to the pastor and the congregation. The news was well received, and today we serve the community of Olanchito."
(Siris Santiago)

Those words were for me!

"God called me to missions in the Republic of Peru in 1988. It happened during a short-term trip with "CONFRA" from the University of Puerto Rico. On the last day of the trip, it was my turn to preach, and I was touched by my own message. I felt the call when I quoted Philippians 3:7-8, "But whatever gain I had, I counted as loss for the sake of Christ. And indeed, I count all things but loss for the excellency of the knowledge of Christ Jesus my Lord, for whom I have suffered the loss of all things, and count them but dung, that I may win Christ." Those words were for me! After finishing the reflection, I came down from the altar to pray and in tears, I promised the Lord that I would return to Peru and do His will.

Fifteen years of preparation passed without really understanding God's plan. I returned with several groups of short-term mission trips helping evangelical churches in the expansion of the gospel in their communities. The short trips were characterized by services in different locations and interacting with national pastors in evangelism in the capital, northern, jungle and highlands of Peru. Simultaneously, my husband and I prepared ourselves for missions in a school and with a mission agency, without ceasing to serve in our local church in Puerto Rico. In 2006, together with my family, we began to serve full time as church planters." (Evelyn Centeno)

Your plan is better

"For my thoughts are not your thoughts, neither are your ways my ways, saith the LORD. As the heavens are higher than the earth, so are my ways higher than your ways, and my thoughts than your thoughts." Isaiah 55:8-9, Reina-Valera 1960

"I met the Lord when I was fourteen years old. And because of this relationship with God, I asked Him to direct me toward what I should study when it came time to select a college.   To my understanding I was directed toward a career in criminology and criminal law. I began to like this career more than I thought I would and began to make my own plans. I had it all figured out. When I finished, I would seek to work in some federal investigative agency, while completing a master's degree in the same field of study... until I learned about the persecuted church and the unreached.

God, using preaching, reading books and other means, began to confront me. What was I doing at that time in my life while there were so many brothers giving their lives for the cause of Jesus? What was I doing while there were people who longed to have access to the Word of God in their language and did not have it? And I was not seeking Him as I was supposed to. This confrontation led me to value His Word even more.

God made me understand that everything I was questioning about the career, it was really because I was so eager to pursue the profession. I thought that was why God took me to study it. But I was only thinking about getting a job according to the earthly world. So, the Holy Spirit was working in me. God was taking away my "chip" and putting on His, completely transforming my vision and depositing His in me, ceasing to visualize myself working in some agency and seeing myself serving in the church.

I continued to study more about persecution through the Scriptures, until the day came when I told the Lord: "With my life I want to please You, I want to work for Your kingdom, for the glory and honor of Your name, not mine. I want to dedicate my life to You, to Your service, to the expansion of Your kingdom. I want to work for the expansion of Your kingdom from the time I get up until the time I go to bed. Let whatever I do bring glory to Your name, not mine." From that point on, it was God directing me toward "His plan."

About three years passed when I completed my degree in college. Around that same time, I learned about an opportunity to serve in the area of Bible translation. I remember that first day of the workshop when they talked about what it was all about and the reality of Bible translation. I was stunned and my heart wanted to burst out of my chest. I thought, "How is it possible that there are still so many ethnic groups that don't have the Bible? It can't be!" I knew there was a need, but I had no idea of the magnitude. I continued to participate in workshops and the Lord gave me the opportunity to have my first experience in the field with this ministry. It was there, having that direct contact with indigenous people, where God confirmed to me that it was in the field, full time where He wanted me.

I am currently serving in Paraguay. I participated in a workshop for exegetes and a consulting session under the guidance of a biblical consultant, after which I have begun to help in the exegetical revision of the translations. So far, I had only participated in the first stage of the whole translation process, in that part of the initial draft, but now I was seeing the other side of the coin, the exegetical revision part. Seeing the work live and in full color, I was realizing that this is my place. I was seeing how I was somehow fitting what I had studied in the secular world. Well, for this exegetical part you have to be very meticulous, you have to dig and investigate, which I had learned while studying, and this was precisely the area that I was passionate about in my career. So, the more I get involved, the more the Lord confirms to me that this is my part in His plan, in His kingdom. To collaborate for the rest of my life for the fulfillment of Revelation 7:9 where it says that every nation, tribe, people, and tongue will cry out with a loud voice, saying, "Salvation belongs to our God who sits on the throne, and to the Lamb." (Yarimar Ruiz)

I know Christ Will make a way for me...

"I felt that God was trying to tell me something and He sought to do it with much love and affection, like that of a Father. He precisely used my earthly father, whom I loved so much, to bring me back to His ways. In the loving way that God dealt with me, so did my father and this caused me to reconcile my relationship with the Lord after a while. The Word was already there in my mind and in my heart. After I reconciled with the Lord, I felt more mature and wanted to get answers from the Bible as my mother had sought. Many people unknowingly began to influence my life. One in particular, Lucy, was introducing me to the field of cross-cultural missions. Thank you, for letting me use Lucy! But the Word of God had convinced me that God wanted to reach all the people of the earth through Jesus Christ.

I didn't feel called to serve on the mission field, but I began to study at the school of missions; and every course I attended was like a refreshment. There, I was inspired by the lives of many people who had served Christ on the mission field.

One day, while taking a literacy course at the mission school, I was disturbed when the teacher, my friend and mentor, Tali, began to sing a song in the Yagüa language of Peru. I didn't know what the meaning was, but I knew there was a message for me. I asked her the meaning and she began to sing it in Spanish: "I know that Christ will make a way for me. And if I live in holiness, He will guide me; I know that Christ will make a way for me." What did you think I did? I began to cry. What would that way be? I wanted to know.

Soon the time came when I no longer wanted to attend any more mission congresses or short cross-cultural experience trips like the ones I had attended. Now I want to go! God called me to go! It just so happened that one day when I was doing my personal morning devotions, I was reading Isaiah 42 when I felt the Lord speak to me through verses 6 and 7. These spoke of how God calls His suffering Servant and takes him by the hand. I wondered, "Why, as I read about the Suffering Servant, did I feel the Lord calling me to serve in a task?" It is those moments when you know you are in the presence of the Lord. I felt that God took me by the hand, and He did. What I did not understand was how or in what way I was going to do what it says in Isaiah 42, for the Suffering Servant is the Lord and He gave sight to the blind, brought prisoners out of prison... He already suffered and made a sacrifice for me.

But what was I to do? Then He began to guide me along the path He had for me, with many challenges, but which have affirmed me in my calling. God set the stage with opportunities that allowed me to develop the skills I would need to become involved in linguistics, literacy, and translation ministry. Currently, along with another colleague in ministry, we are supporting a group originally from Mexico in creating literacy and linguistics materials, translating the New Testament and promoting the use of the mother tongue." (Marian)

You will go to Spain...

"I had gone through the experience of a divorce. And now I was a single mother and head of a family with two teenagers and a baby girl. It was a night of evangelistic campaign in the nascent church, still considered a preaching point of the ICDC[17] in PR in the residential area of El Señorial. The preacher invited us to come forward to pray...all with our heads down in prayer and eyes closed. Suddenly, I heard an audible voice say to me, "You will go to Spain." I raised my head, opened my eyes, and saw no one around me speaking. This came as a total surprise to me. How could I go to Spain in the midst of the crisis of my recent divorce, with three children, and a job to attend to? I told my pastors what had happened, and they very wisely suggested that I continue praying. But I did not sit idly by and started studying at the Betania School of Missions and participated in several exploratory trips to Spain. It was there that my passion for the Missions and for Spain began. I began with passion to pray for Galicia, my passion was the ethnic group of the Galicians. I felt that the Holy Spirit was directing me there". *(María Toro)*

It is time to sow...

"I was 24 years old when I felt the Lord's call to go to Italy. I came to this country to specialize in my psychology studies, but God had other plans in store for me in this nation.

In the past I had accepted my call to missions, when the Lord had impressed upon my heart the verse from Isaiah 6:8:

---

[17] Iglesia Cristiana Discípulos de Cristo.

Then I heard the voice of the Lord saying, whom shall I send, and who will go for us? And I answered, here am I, send me! At that moment, just like Isaiah, I answered, "Here am I, send me." I knew this call was for me and without hesitation I responded. Then I received confirmation of my calling for Italy also by the Word of God. Once again, God put a verse from the book of Isaiah on my heart, in this case Isaiah 55:5: "Behold, you shall call a nation that you have not known, and nations that have not known you shall run to you, for the sake of the LORD your God, and of the Holy One of Israel who has honored you." So strong in me was the conviction of my calling to this country, that I came to Italy, where I have served for more than thirty years.

I have dedicated my life, my strength, and resources to carry the message to this nation in every possible way. It was necessary for me to work secularly in this country because I was one of the first missionaries sent from my country, the Dominican Republic, and the responsibility of economic support to the missionaries was not well understood. On the other hand, this has been one of the doors to communicate the Gospel, where I preach not only with my word, but also with my testimony. On more than one occasion, the Italians have told me: "But what are you doing here? You came because in your country there is no work, there is a shortage of food. And with love I explained to them that I was there to communicate to them the message of love and salvation through Jesus Christ. Following the Lord's call has cost me to leave my family, friends, and a good economic position. But it has all been worth it.

God has helped me to persevere and not get discouraged. Italy has been considered the cemetery of the missionaries; and not seeing many fruits like the ones one expects, brings much discouragement. For this reason, many have left the field, but the Lord has spoken to me clearly: "Mariela, now is the time to sow! You are sowing...! And in due time we will reap if we do not lose heart!" And so, it has been. In the first years very few people were converted, but in obedience I kept on sowing. My husband and I are pastors of a mother church founded in 2003, in the City of Parma, with a membership of 150 to 200 people. Seven years ago, we founded a second church in the City of Fidenza, 25 km from Parma, which we oversee, but already has pastors and leaders. At the moment we are starting another church in Reggio Emilia, 30 km from Parma, and a white field in Cuneo, Piemonte, 300 km from Parma. (Mariela de los Santos)

There is room for everyone

"In the classroom I looked out, and there in the near distance were several nuns from my school doing some work. An attraction to spiritual things was growing stronger and stronger in me. It was the 80's, in that town of Luque, Paraguay, when God began to touch my heart. Due to the beginning of the civil war in my country, El Salvador, my family moved to Paraguay.

God used this trip to transform our lives. Before traveling, we were nominal Christians of the traditional religion. Upon arriving in Paraguay, my sister and I were enrolled in the nearest Catholic school; but my brother had been enrolled in the city of Asuncion, in a Baptist school. It was for this reason that he and my mother decided to visit the small Baptist church in our community. It was love at first sight! God worked quickly, and in a short time, almost all of us had been impacted by the message of salvation in Jesus Christ! The following year, we returned to El Salvador, only my brother Erwing remained in Paraguay to finish his high school.

In the beginning of my adult life, I was part of a family business that my sister Beatriz and I managed. Those years helped me to start putting my career into practice. I got married and my first son, Daniel, was born. After several years we closed the company and I told the Lord that I wanted to serve Him in some ministry, I did not know where, I began to search on my own, but to no avail. It was then that I received an invitation to collaborate as a volunteer in a local missionary agency. It was necessary to participate in the Perspectives course and there was one in progress, with teachers from all over the continent. Since I started the course, God was speaking to my life, and I almost wanted to raise my hand and go as a missionary. But that was not what God had for me.

During a class break, one of the lecturers gave me a sticker, which read, "Move your life in this direction. Wycliffe." And I asked, "What's Wycliffe?" "It's the Bible translators," someone else told me. It all still sounded like Chinese to me, but it would change my whole life from then on. From that moment on, it was like the words "Bible translation" spoke to me in every text that mentioned them.

At that same time my marriage ended. I had been left with my five-year-old son, a tough ordeal, which I never imagined I would go through. But I had learned to pray and fast during the crisis, and to trust God for my future. We were in His hands. I began to ask the Lord for a family, because I did not want to be a single mother all my life.

Later, a group of missionaries who had been in Papua New Guinea visited the agency for a Prayer Concert. In the middle of their presentation, they projected videos about the need to translate the Word of God in that place, where there are more than 800 languages and many of them do not have the Bible in their language. Suddenly, it was as if rivers of tears were flowing from inside me, and I had to go out to cry and talk to the Lord. I was saying, "What do you want from me, Lord, I am divorced, how can I serve you?" At the end of the presentation, I went to talk to the guys, and I told them what had just happened to me. They encouraged me by saying that there is room for everyone in service to the Lord! My excitement was great. Now I understood why Brother Adelmo Ruiz had given me that sticker months ago.

Soon after, I participated in a training for mobilizers, which was the first time it was given in the region. From that training, together with other beloved brothers, TRES (Bible Translators of El Salvador) was born. I embraced the vision of starting a Bible translation project for every town without a Bible (Vision 2025), and we began to spread information. We visited churches, held orientation workshops about Bible translation and began to connect with brethren from other

*countries in the region. But that was not all God had for me..."
(Olivia Jaime de Serrano)*

God used my pride to trap me

"I didn't see angels, I didn't hear an audible voice, I didn't feel anything in my heart, nor had I gone out to other countries. I was in the wrong room. I had been baptized months before, I had been converted for a year, so I was on cloud nine, in my first love, but still with some things to work on, like pride. Every year my church assigned tasks or roles to people to collaborate or work in the church. I, being new, had signed up to help in the kitchen. After telling everyone where they were going to work, they set up a day of meetings in which everyone had to go to the room of the work committee to which they had been assigned. I went into the room and since there were already a lot of people in the room, it was my turn to sit at the end of the room.   There I arrived, very proud, because I was going to serve God.

As soon as two more entered the room, they closed the door and the person at the front introduced himself and said: "Thank you all for being here and accepting this challenge. Almost all of us are already members of this team and we have to quickly discuss the activity we have at the end of the month, the evangelistic campaign to Mayagüez (a town in the west of the island) where we will stay all weekend. What? What are you talking about? What activity are you talking about?

As I continued listening to what the brother was saying, I realized something.   I had the wrong room.   That was the mission committee room. I had made a mistake. But my pride got the better of me. How are you going to stand up in the middle of the meeting and walk out of the room? How are you going to tell them that you have the wrong room? You want to be embarrassed? Unbelievable, God used my pride to keep me in the missions committee room, which I haven't left in 27 years. (Wendy)

Necessity... a call to missions

Sometimes God has practical ways of showing us that we can do something for missions. Sometimes He lets us see a need, He makes us understand that our academic preparation was for a divine purpose. In short, He lets us know that there is work to be done and that He prepares us to serve without excuses.

I can't just sit on my hands

"My son-in-law Amaury Blondet and my youngest daughter Cristina Collazo Toro founded an NGO called Planeta Feliz. They have been working in Haiti since 2008, before the 2010 earthquake. He had to take a trip to the south of the island, to Anse-a-Pitres, Haiti, and I accompanied him. It was August 2011. That first visit took my breath away - so much poverty, and we had so many resources. Us, with so many resources, what can I do? "I can't sit on my hands," I told the Lord. We were only there for about four days, but upon my return I continued to pray for so much need. In April

2012, I left Puerto Rico to stay south of the Island of Hispaniola, divided by a river that marks the border between the Dominican Republic and the Republic of Haiti." (Maria Toro, 2012-2020)

"This is your place."

"This is your place", that was the voice of God that I heard inside me in 1982, on my first short-term mission trip to a place in Colombia, called Monteria. From that moment on, every testimony I heard from missionaries at missionary conferences, every song alluding to missions, the teachings of my pastor Rev. Terranova, and the Word of God, quickened my heart and confirmed the call I had received.

I understood that in order to go to that "place" called Missions and answer that call, I had to prepare myself. At the end of my career as an accountant at the University of Puerto Rico, I entered the Theological Seminary of the Christian and Missionary Alliance, where I was one of the first graduates of the Master of Divinity Program.

After twelve years of preparation in different areas, both biblical and theological, as well as family and emotional, on February 13, 1994 I left my beautiful little island, Puerto Rico, for an adventure of faith called "missions." In these twenty-five years I have lived in three countries that have been "my place" of Missions, although I have visited and taught in many other countries in Latin America. When I reflect on the words of that call thirty-seven years ago, 'I have understood that it did not refer to a specific geographic location, but to a "place" in God's missionary work.'" (Maritza Cumba)

A growing passion

"Since my conversion in 1990, I had the opportunity to serve in different areas in the church in Venezuela. I remember it was there, in a meeting of teenagers, that for the first time God spoke to me "that He would take me to many nations." At that time, I had no idea how that was going to happen. It wasn't until years later that the Lord began to speak to me more clearly about a missionary calling. Through different ministers of His, and in different places, they spoke to me not only about the call but also that God would use me through my profession as an administrator, which He has done. It should be noted that I did not know any of these people that God used to give me some prophetic word about what He wanted to do with me. The Lord knows us well and knows how to deal with each of His children, and in my case, to put aside any skepticism, when He used these people, they confirmed something He had already told me on another occasion. On each occasion, they offered me more details about the missionary call, to the point that there was no longer any doubt about it. In addition to a passion that grew more and more, I read, researched on my own, and prayed for the unreached peoples, especially for those in the West African region, a region that occupies a special place in my heart.

It was not until 2009 that I decided to quit my formal job to dedicate myself to serve the Lord full time and launch into the adventure of beginning to learn to live in absolute dependence on the Lord. Definitely, I saw how from this decision God accelerated my steps. I began to work in an office schedule in the administration of my church. Surprisingly, they decided to give me a monthly offering for my service in the church, with which I paid part of my studies in theology. I collaborated with the development of the mission's program in the church and served two years on the board of SIETE (a movement that promotes Bible translation and literacy among the Venezuelan ethnic groups).

In my journey to the field, I had to overcome some obstacles such as fear, the disbelief of some, the doubt, the uncertainty of how this would happen in what we have never been involved in, among others. They were overcome with much prayer and faith in what God had promised. It is then that, under the blessing of my pastors, the support of my church and family, and my recent graduation in Theology at SEPAD (Evangelical Seminary of the Assemblies of God), in the city of Barquisimeto-Venezuela in September 2011, I was part of the first cross-cultural missionary training launched by Mundo Horizontes Venezuela. This training was aimed at Venezuelans who were ready to be sent to less evangelized nations... It was the "EDIFICA Project", and through which I had the opportunity to reach West Africa and serve with one of our teams for two years. It was a time of dedication, passionate service and integral growth." (Katiusca Lilibeth Ibarra Ron)

I have to do something else, please use me...

"At the age of twelve I first heard about the unreached peoples. These unreached places were beyond the borders of my country. But without hesitating for a minute, I said to the Lord, "I have to do something else, please use me."

One day my pastor from Nicaragua invited a pastor from Costa Rica to come to the first missions conference the church would have. We were all looking forward to what this new challenge was all about. Finally, the expected day arrived. We began hearing amazing and wonderful testimonies of what God was doing in other towns, but also that there was a long way to go before the task was finished and that there were not many who were willing to go to these places.

Pastor Denis asked my pastor if he would allow me to wear a Muslim woman's dress on the last day of our conference, but he pointed out that no one in the congregation could know it was me. That Sunday I got up very early to go to the Pastor's house and from there we would leave for church in a black suit that covered my entire body and face. To literally be in the shoes and dress of one of these women impacted my heart. We got into a cab and at once I grabbed the attention of the cab driver, and he began to ask: who is she? Does she always have to be dressed like that? What nationality is she? In short, all the questions we could imagine. The ride was short. Over there my presence also caused another impact. People wanted to know who I was. They wanted to shake my hand, but I could only respond with a nod of my head. I could not answer their questions. Being at least five hours under that black veil where it seemed I was a wall and that did not allow me to be close to people, made me feel isolated. I was limited in expressing what I felt, which struck my heart. But there I was saying to the Lord, "I can do something more for these people."

God heard my prayer and allowed me to serve in a beautiful project focused on the prevention of human trafficking, a very common problem in this world today and one that greatly affects the Asian region, where God sent me. We started with the Perla project, to alert the community about the issue. But the Lord asked us to go to the next level, so He put on the heart of one of my co-workers a project for a sewing center. The goal of this was to help women who have been trafficked and other women who were not trafficked, so that they can survive by working in sewing. So, we have addressed not only the spiritual need, but also the economic need of these women. I am deeply grateful to God for bringing me to Southeast Asia, where He has allowed me to serve Him already for eight years." (Elba Bermudez)

Anywhere but in the missions

"I received the call to serve the Lord in missions in 1991. My oldest son was one month old at the time. At that time, I was serving in my local church as a youth leader and Sunday school teacher. In my local church we had been taught a lot about serving the Lord. I often expressed how much I wanted to serve the Lord, but I always told Him that I would serve Him in anything but missions. I admired the missionaries, but it seemed to me that I could not leave my country and leave my family. That seemed very difficult to me to achieve, so I had "been specific" with Him. Oops! It turned out that His plans were different for me.

My husband at the time was a national youth leader in our denomination, and he was invited to attend a missionary convention, which was called Commitment 2000. A colleague invited him insistently and my husband, to get out of the way, decided to go one day. That day changed his life, because for the first time he heard about the unreached. He learned about the thousands of people who had not heard about Jesus in countries were going as a traditional missionary was impossible. He learned that with our professions we could enter to serve in these places.

I remember that when he arrived home, he told me everything he had heard in that activity and after that we began to attend some meetings of young professionals with a missionary vision. There we met people with a call to missions to the unreached, who were preparing to go out to the field with their profession. These future missionaries needed support, so my husband and I said, "Well, we are definitely not going out, because we will be the ones who support others to go."

One day our pastor asked us to organize our church's mission week. We thought, "Let's organize this missionary week in the best way we can, so that when the week is over, many will say they want to go out to the field to serve the Lord." We had people invited; and we also thought of projecting a movie. We didn't know much about missionary movies, so in procuring the movie I said, "I want you to recommend a movie about missions, that when the movie is over all the people will end up crying and say I want to go." Imagine what kind of movie I was asking for. Rodolfo told me, "I have that movie." So, without seeing it before and just trusting his recommendation the movie was shown in the church. And what do you think? When the movie was over, the one who was telling the Lord with tears that I would serve Him in missions, was me!

So, when He called me, I cried a lot, because it was not something I wanted to do.   I knew it meant leaving my country and my family, but also in my heart I knew I could not disobey the Lord and His call.   That day I cried a lot, I cried expressing to my husband about my experience.   To my surprise the Lord had already called my husband to missions, but he had not told me. As a result, in 1997 we left for the mission field where we have spent twenty-three years serving the Lord among the unreached in Muslim countries." (Abigail Forero)[18]

Let them sit and wait!

"I am Ivonne Seguí, born in Puerto Rico. For family reasons, from an early age we moved for a while to the United States, to New York City. It was there where I had my encounter with the Lord, where I decided to give my life to Him, at the approximate age of fourteen to fifteen years old. At that time, I became involved in different areas of the church. Together with my parents I began to study the Word. I remember that God, at some point through some preacher who visited the church, told me that He had a ministry for me. At that time, I did not understand what he was talking about.

---

[18] Pseudonym

When we moved to Puerto Rico in 1975, we joined the church in the town where we went to live. Little by little I assumed responsibilities in the church. There I grew and matured spiritually. The Lord was speaking to my life about callings, but I still did not understand. I even had pastors who said that they saw me in some country as a missionary, to which I answered to myself: "Let them sit and wait!"

For me, missions were something unthinkable. I had very wrong concepts about them, as a result of the testimonies I had heard since my childhood, testimonies that emphasized scarcity, eating strange things, suffering, etc., and I was not willing to do that.

In Puerto Rico I finished my high school, I studied at the University, business administration with a major in accounting. When I finished my academic career, I started working in a very well-known manufacturing company. It was a real blessing! God used that job to help me change my character and where I had the opportunity to travel to other places. Unbeknownst to me, God was preparing me to be away from my family.

I began to hear other things about missions, including a short trip to Venezuela. Within my organization there was a program where they talked about how you could serve with your talents, abilities, and preparation. It was at that time that I began to contemplate the idea of missions. There was a need for a secretary in Bible colleges in Europe, and I was attracted to the idea. At that time, I met up with a friend who had gone to Peru as a missionary. She was back in Puerto Rico and was starting a missionary ministry called El Shaddai. In it, they organized short-term mission trips to support the missionaries in the field. As I shared with her my concerns about what God had spoken to me, my mind became more open to missions. That year, 1990, El-Shaddai Ministries was traveling to Spain. My friend asked me, "When will you travel with us?" I replied, "Whenever I feel like it." Then, thinking about the conversation, when I got home, I wrote to her asking her for the travel information. But she, before receiving my letter, was already sending me the information. Coincidence?

That was how I found myself attending the meetings in preparation for the trip, but still feeling unsure about participating in it. Could it be God's will? I had no financial obstacles, nor work permits. I just wasn't sure whether or not it was His will. Until, in one of the meetings, God spoke to me so clearly that my doubts were dispelled. He told me: "I have put you here for help, it will be the beginning of many things". With that assurance I arrived in Spain. My heart was captivated by that congregation, and by seeing so much need for help. I thought about how much we, as a Puerto Rican church, could contribute to that country. That trip changed my heart. So much so, that I returned two more summers, and on a third occasion, it was for a prolonged period of time. But it wasn't all as fast as we sometimes think it will be. With each trip the call in me for that country grew more and more and God confirmed His will in my life. So it was that in 1993 I arrived in Spain with the idea of staying for a year. That's what I thought, but at the time of writing this I have been here for twenty-seven years". (Ivonne Seguí, Spain)

Different calls, different missionaries

"They shall not build for another to dwell in, nor plant for another to eat; for according to the days of the trees shall be the days of My people, and My chosen ones shall enjoy the work of their hands." Isaiah 65:22 Reina-Valera 1960 (RVR1960)

There are some jobs in missions, which we could say are not traditional. People have been taught that their professions are to generate income for a living. On the other hand, in the churches it has been taught that to serve in missions you have to leave your country and live in another country, but nothing could be more wrong in this time in which we live. God wants us to serve Him in missions with everything, even with our professions. He wants us to enjoy what we do for Him, and what better than doing for God what we know and like to do? So, we can find many women serving in a different, but no less important way in missions today.

Serving in mobilization

"And how shall they preach unless they are sent? As it is written, ``How beautiful are the feet of them that preach peace, of them that bring glad tidings of good things!" Romans 10:15 Reina-Valera 1960 (RVR1960)

"I worked in several places under the Public Residential Administration in Puerto Rico. This gave me the opportunity to get to know different populations and with varied needs. I saw in many of those I served the pain, the

extreme poverty, the injustice, the difference in treatment according to social levels, the violence between sides, the abuse. But, on the other hand, I also met very good and humble people there. In my work, the Lord taught me to manage and work with all these populations. Now I understand that all that route along which the Lord was leading me was for the purpose of being able to serve as I do today.

God was preparing me even without my knowing it. I went through many trials, but it was all part of the process. One day I began to dream; something that had not happened to me in years. These dreams began to be very frequent, and the strangest thing was that I would dream of the same thing several nights in a row. At the same time, an opportunity arose for me to take a trip to Israel. When I arrived there, I realized that everything I had dreamed about was the same thing that actually happened on my trip. This made me very upset; I was afraid that the Lord was telling me to do something, and I could not figure out what it was. I am still waiting to understand where and where God wants to take me, because I understand that I am still in the process of preparation.

Now, trying to know his will, I keep looking for him. I joined the missions committee of my local church, where I later became the president. I began to study the Bible in a theological college, I participated in seminars, lectures, workshops, everything that would lead me to know more about God and his mission, in order to serve him. It is on one of these occasions that I learned about the AMIES association. Along with the mission's ministry of my church, I began to visit the association and I was excited about the idea of serving with

124

them, to get to know more fully other missionaries or people who loved and were enthusiastic about what I was most interested in, "missions". As soon as I finished my studies, I joined the agency to help in everything I could. At that time the secretary resigned, and I was assigned to that position. Later on, the director's position became vacant, and they offered me the position, since they knew my work and ministerial experience. Currently, I serve there, where the mission is to mobilize the missionary vision and help the missionaries that go out to the field, so from here I serve every nation. God prepared me for this time." (Magdalena Cotto, Puerto Rico)

But it was not yet complete...

"I still didn't feel complete, I was working for the Lord, but I was alone with my five-year-old son. I kept praying, crying out to the Lord for a husband who could share my passion to serve Him, who would love me, and also my son, and God granted it!!!! Jorge came into my life at the right time planned by God. We met in the office of TRES[19] (the organization with which I collaborated). God had a work in store for us, together. In 2015, Jorge joined the TRES team and that same year we got married.

"But without faith it is impossible to please God: for he that cometh to God must believe that he is, and that he is a rewarder of them that diligently seek him." Hebrews 11:6

---

[19] Traductores Bíblicos de El Salvador, an organization that offers training in linguistics, anthropology and literacy. It is also dedicated to mobilizing for Bible Translation.

Jorge and I are living testimonies of the prayer of faith. For many years he had prayed for a wife, after going through a separation, as had I. I prayed for almost three years. I prayed almost three years .... for what I can now share with you who read these lines, there is nothing impossible for God! Have faith! God has given us together two precious children, Olivia and Joshua, who, together with Daniel and Jorge Jr. completed our quiver.

This is how God has continued the work, for together, during the fifteen years of marriage, we have traveled thousands of miles, serving the Lord in mobilizing for Bible translation, organizing workshops, courses, meeting wonderful people who have taken the vision. We participate in the elaboration of prayer bulletins, coordinate the prayer area of A Toda Lengua, and other efforts. We also collaborate in the development of promotional materials, manuals, creating content for more churches to participate in the precious ministry of Bible translation.

We serve with passion in several organizations. After serving in TRES for some years, God called us to serve Him at the continental level, working with COMIBAM and then with Wycliffe Global Alliance Americas and collaborating with other like-minded organizations. It was a privilege to serve the Lord in the organization "responsible" for my calling and ministry.

But God's work in us and through us was not yet complete. A few years ago, God was making us restless to spread our tent by continuing in missionary mobilization, but no longer only for Bible translation.   Although the Bibleless peoples are still in our hearts beating strongly, we began to move toward strategic prayer in a more global way, on behalf of the persecuted church, the refugees, and the unreached.

At the same time, God has led us to make other changes.   Since 2016, God has brought us back to the corporate world because He always has purposes in all our movements.   There, I realized that it is also necessary to serve God as bi-occupational workers, and yes, I can do that.   We serve the Lord now with the gifts in the professions He has given us, Law and Marketing, but He has also allowed us to continue serving Him in His work.   God has led us to knock on doors of entrepreneurs who can "give" for His mission and allow us to experience new ways of participating in missionary mobilization."   (Olivia Jaime de Serrano)

Go and tell them...

"For ten years I was the chairman of the missions committee of my church and as part of my responsibilities I would attend missions' events to bring information to the church to get the church more involved in missions.   There were also people on my team who had expressed concern about some particular areas of missions and one of them was the issue of Bible translation.   At the insistence of a member of my team, I wrote to Wycliffe USA to request information on this topic.   In response, they told me that there was going to be a conference in Puerto Rico on the subject on two Saturdays.   So, I wrote requesting the information of the specific place and I

spoke to my mission team of the church so that those who wanted to accompany me could do so.

The expected Sabbath arrived and from the moment I entered the conference room I felt something hit my heart. There was a big list on the wall. A list with more than three thousand names of people without a Bible, representing millions and millions of people. After several hours at the event and watching a movie, I stood in front of that list. I began to cry thinking how grateful I was that someone had translated the Bible into Spanish and that we were not on that list. I couldn't stop crying. Like all women, and in a society where we have been taught that women should always look good, I remembered that I had makeup on my eyes and that everything was probably smudged from tears. I reached for my purse, which was just brand new, which had a small mirror in it. But when I looked in the mirror to clean myself up and make sure it looked good, I couldn't see myself clearly. Repeatedly I tried to look in the mirror, until I noticed something. The mirror of my new wallet has transparent protective paper over it. For that reason, I didn't look good; I was looking at myself in the paper and not in the mirror. So, I carefully peeled it off. But imagine, as soon as I removed this paper, I heard the voice of God in my heart saying to me, "Just as you didn't see well, my church doesn't see well either. They don't know that there are people without a Bible. Go and tell them." As you can imagine, then I cried more, God was sending me on a mission. One that was the beginning of my life in the Bible translation ministry exercising many roles and reaching many countries, but most of all telling everyone that there are still Bibleless Peoples, and it is up to us to help translate it as they once did for us." (Wendy)

Doing Theology in the Field

When we live, work, and breathe missions.   We are doing nothing other than practicing theology. However, often these two words are not found in the same sentence. Theology arises from the daily life in which Christians live their faith in relation to everything: poverty, violence, uncertainty, lack of health services and everything that affects every human being. This is what Latin missionary women live daily in the places where they serve.

Mission is not just going, giving and receiving passively, but rather it is touching and influencing the history of the communities where the mission takes place. But in order to do this, and being careful not to fall into syncretism, missions must consider the culture when transmitting the gospel. "The gospel by principle is distinct from culture, but it cannot be separated from it, because it uses cultural expressions as a vehicle to manifest itself." [20]

The gospel that is lived is translated from one culture to another.[21] Just as God became incarnate to bring his message to our human reality, in the person of Jesus Christ. But how do the people in the fields where these Latina missionaries serve see Jesus Christ? As Jesus asked his disciples: Who do men say that the Son of Man is?[22] Knowing the answer to this question is indispensable for the missionaries, in order to be able to develop a plan of action or work that helps them to understand the redemptive work of Jesus Christ. This redemptive work of Jesus Christ has been interpreted in different ways: Jesus as payment for sin; as a saving example; as a conqueror; and as the head of a new humanity.[23] Knowing these interpretations and the way in which they see or know Jesus in the community they serve, offers the missionaries in the field a basis for all ministry and/or strategy

---

[20] Paul Cardinal Poupard, "Evangelio y Cultura: En los Umbrales del Tercer Milenio", Trabajo presentado, Universidad La Sapienza, Roma, 26 de mayo de 1998, 6.

[21] González, *Historia General de las Misiones, 309.*

[22] Mateo 16:13, Reina-Valera 1960 (RVR1960).

[23] Justo L. González & Zaida Maldonado Pérez, *Introducción a la Teología Cristiana*, 82-87.

that they develop, seeking that all actions provoke God to reveal Jesus Christ as He revealed Him to Peter.

All theology is contextual,[24] Therefore, every person called to the missions must know everything that surrounds her in her new community. It is only by knowing how they think and what they think in that community, that the missionaries have been able to achieve results in their efforts. They have developed a practical theology that has provoked the transformation of lives, and even of some communities, as is the case of those who work with nutrition education, and the denunciation of human trafficking, as platforms to carry the message of justice, love and mercy. They have understood that it is in the heart of the community where theology is done.[25]

In the missions we sometimes speak of inculturation, which is much more than the adaptation of the Christian faith to a people. It is rather living and expressing Christian convictions in new ways, starting from the roots of the culture being served. But to achieve these expressions one must first know the values and worldview of the people. One must know the answers to questions such as: What do they understand sin to be? Where do they find salvation? Do they believe in life beyond death? The answers to these questions help the missionaries to find creative ways, not only to present the Nazarene, but also to help them grow in their relationship with God in a healthy and biblical way.

---

[24] González, *Introducción a la Teología Cristiana,* (Nashville: Abingdon Press, 1998), *27.*

[25] González, *Introducción a la Teología Cristiana,* 24.

But why is it important to know these answers beyond a work plan? Well, because they are elements of the Christian faith, which help people in the fields to recognize the work of Jesus Christ and to respond to him in love and repentance. In places like Mexico, where they see Jesus as a statue that is carried on pilgrimages, but they worship the image without understanding that they can have a personal relationship with God, it is important to understand where this belief comes from. How can we make them understand that this statue of Christ on the cross is not the end? Let them understand that Christ is the victor, even though he was also the sacrifice and that for that reason it is not necessary to make more sacrifices, as many still believe necessary.

How to say that Jesus Christ paid the price for the sin of a community that does not believe that sin exists? How to make the marginalized understand that, even if they have nothing to offer, God loves them? How to tell an Italian that, even if he is Italian and Catholic, he needs the salvation of his soul and a personal relationship with God? How to help converts to resist going back to the customs of their ancestors, practiced for centuries? How to make them understand that, although Jesus Christ is historical, he is real and true today too? How to show people how to live the whole life that God wants, even outside of religious structures? The answers to these questions have definitely been the strategies that the Holy Spirit has inspired and continues to inspire Latina women in the field, strategies that are flexible, that exhibit God's gifts in them, along with the ability these women have to adapt to different environments.

Today the mission of the church is fulfilled in the midst of a great diversity of cultures on all continents. This makes it all the more necessary to pray and turn to God to respond with discernment and wisdom to intercultural and interreligious phenomena. It is therefore of utmost importance that every woman and man with a call to missions should be educated in both the spiritual disciplines and in the knowledge of the Word of God, which together will increase the impact of their witness. The professional formation that those called to missions may have is an added ingredient that in some cases will offer the missionary privileged places where they could impact more lives, and therefore a greater reach in the communities.

God has trained and called hundreds of Latina women to missions who have a great capacity to adapt, to try to transmit the values of the kingdom in the best possible way. Some are women who have been discarded by others, but who have been empowered by God and by the experiences they have lived. They are widows, single and married women, with and without children, who understand the commitment to accompany people in the search for truth. They are women who have been marginalized by organizations or by society itself, but whom God has called to carry His message with a deep knowledge of the faith, acquired from their own experiences. They serve a world that is full of tensions, which demand acts of faith, love and hope.

Each person who comes in contact with a missionary has her own story, and women in missions have the call to touch those lives with the mantle of the Master so that His miracle may occur. Elba tells us one of the many wonderful stories of life transformation of one of the women who live inside the sewing center, whom we will call Joy.

"She is a woman of approximately 30 years of age. She is the third child of five siblings. When she was very young, her family left the island, where they were originally from, to live on another island. Seeking a better life, she decides to move to the capital where she thought she would find more work options, but there she meets a man whom she decides to marry, without her family's blessing or approval. The man she married was a Muslim. After her marriage she moved to a smaller town near the capital, but here her family began to pressure her to leave her husband, even though she was pregnant at the time with the man's baby. The pressure was such that she abandoned him and returned to the capital, losing all contact with him to this day.

She went to live at a friend's house. She left her child with her to go to work at a clothing stand. Her friend told her that the salary she received was very little, that she could not help her much, but she told her that she knew a place where she could work and receive a higher salary than the current one. The place was a "café" (this is how some prostitution centers are called and they are also called "Karaoke"). It was there that she began her life in the world of prostitution. Unfortunately, in this job she contracted an illness, which led her to sink into sadness and despair.

It was then that we met Joy and offered to help her. Our team decided to take her in and help her walk to bring hope to her life and that of her little boy, who was only five years old. She is still with us today and always expresses to us that she feels loved, cared for, safe and comfortable, that she feels she has found her refuge and regained her joy. Seeing these transformations in each person's life leaves me speechless. I can only say that it has been worth it to have said to the Father one day: "Here I am, send me". For me it is a privilege to be part of the extension of His Kingdom to the ends of the earth, where I have been able to see the cultural richness, hidden beauties, live in community and where I have been adopted by a family as the youngest sister in the house. I remember His promises to us where He tells us that if we leave our comfort, family, friend, country etc. He will give us more than we have imagined. I can assure you that I have experienced it firsthand, it has been a privilege to invest my life for eternal life." (Elba)

Although Elba does not tell us everything, in order for her to get Joy to come to her, to the ministry and at some point, be sensitive to God's call, Elba had to first see, listen, and learn from Joy's worldview, her family and her community. Elba did not start from nothing, she had to take time in prayer and observation. She had to take time to get to know what was around Joy, in order to introduce her to the Gospel that can change every situation. The Spanish philosopher Jose Ortega y Gasset is well remembered for his expression in a book of Memoirs of Don Quixote where he says, "I am me and my circumstance, and if I do not save her I do not save myself." Elba has not only sought to offer Joy the information for her to decide to accept Jesus Christ as her Savior, but he has also offered her the opportunity for another source of income, impacting everything that is and surrounds Joy.

Like Elba, many of the missionaries serving today have done the same. They have taken time to develop a historical, cultural, and social sensitivity to the population. They do not work in a vacuum. They have had to know not only the geographic location of their work, but also the historical moment of the people they want to reach. To know who they trust, where they seek peace and salvation, whether they believe in it or not. This is not always taught in mission centers or churches; it is learned in the field. Latina women are learning this in the fields, and they are taking advantage of it. As a result of this learning, they are acquiring knowledge that is a key piece to carry the gospel, with strength to be able to transmit it in a way that can be properly interpreted in all cultures.

Latin-American women in the field are offering training, work, food, education, and many other things as expressions of God's presence. Latin-American women in the field are seeking to show Jesus, who some known as only a teacher or a great prophet, for what He is, our Savior and Lord, offering with Him, the hope for a better future that all need.

Christianity has a face of different colors. Women and men of different races and nations declare the wonders of God wherever they go. Latin-American missionaries are some of these faces that have gone to be a voice to the ends of the earth. God continues to call women and men to participate in a movement that recognizes diverse identities but seeks a new

Pentecost, as an introduction to what awaits us in heaven: "After this I looked, and there before me was a great multitude that no one could count, from every nation, tribe, people, and language, standing before the throne and before the Lamb. They were wearing white robes and were holding palm branches in their hands. And they cried out in a loud voice: "Salvation belongs to our God, who sits on the throne, and to the Lamb."

Revelation 7:9-10 New International Version

God has been with Latin-American women in missions, and He has been in the writing of this paper. I was looking for a way to end, but I think Ana Ibel's words are perfect to conclude this work, recognizing that it is only by His grace that we serve and exist. Thank you, God! "It would be unacceptable not to declare that it has been the company of Jesus in my life that has allowed me to do this missionary work. Battles, challenges, struggles, sickness...well, of course they also came on both a personal and ministerial level. The difference was that HIS matchless presence and companionship, comfort and strength allowed the accomplishment of these labors and these experiences, giving faithful testimony of HIS loyalty to those who serve HIM." (Ana Ibel Santiago)

Final words from the missionaries

"Pray in the Spirit at all times and on all occasions. Be alert and persistent in your prayers for all believers everywhere." Ephesians 6:18 NTV

"In our years of service in mission mobilization, our role with my husband has largely been information management to get more people involved in God's mission. When you get informed, God puts a burden, and when you have a burden, you move from pity to compassion, and that leads to action.

And that's because participating in the Great Commission is not an option. It's a mandate. But between the music ministry, the youth ministry, or the Sunday school, which by the way are good, the church does not focus on the remaining task. There is great potential in our churches, but we need to keep informing, motivating the church to participate in praying, giving, promoting, or going.

Today I want to encourage you to pray strategically that you have a missionary map, a globe, photos of the missionaries in your church, that you subscribe to receive information from Bible translation organizations, news of workers, etc. Stay informed of what is happening in the nations to pray! When you pray for someone specific, knowing their needs, or when you pray for an unreached people group knowing how they live and what they need, you are praying strategically. God wants us to come to Him with clear prayer requests, even though He knows everything beforehand.

138

A strategic intercessor goes beyond presenting your personal needs to God. As I write these lines, we find ourselves in the coronavirus pandemic, with as many requests to the Lord as we have ever experienced. Many of them are for protection, for our family and friends. We are living through the hardest times humanity has known in recent times.

But, in spite of the pandemic, I encourage you to extend your eyes and also see the nations in need of Christ. Millions die daily without ever having heard of the gospel of salvation. Millions do not have the Bible in their language, not even having access to John 3:16. Yes, these are millions of people we may never meet, but they are all on God's heart. And our prayers are making a difference!"

Olivia Jaime de Serrano

***

"I encourage and challenge my fellow readers to place their lives, professions and everything they have before the Lord, in order to bring even greater glory to his name and in turn, hope and freedom through Jesus to the lives of thousands of people who do not yet know him.

I invite you to be part of this precious and dignifying work among the most vulnerable. Many more workers are needed, the harvest is ready!"

Elba Bermudez

***

Mariela de los Santos, missionary in Italy advises:

***

"I want to express my gratitude to the following churches that have supported me with their offerings and prayers consecutively for over 15 years: Iglesia Metodista de Puerto Rico, Iglesia Asamblea De Dios El Calvario in Florida and the church Templo Pentecostal in Puerto Rico.

I urge any woman or young person of any age (I arrived after 50) who feels this missionary call, NOT to postpone it. My Lord is the best boss, friend, comforter, and strength that I have had throughout my 18 years of missionary work. Each one of us has special talents that the Lord needs to complete HIS work. Go ahead sisters, the Lord is waiting for us!"

Ana Ibel Santiago

***

"I want to encourage you if you feel your heart burning for missions, respond. The call is the most important thing to have the full assurance of it. The willingness to serve and go where God calls, leaving your friends and family will be an unparalleled experience. But above all, pray and fast to get the discernment and clarity that the rest of your life will be in the hands of the Lord. God bless you!"

Jenny Marcela Cuadros Noriega

140

***

"If you are looking for that place or your life purpose, my advice is to start by loving and serving in your local church with all your heart. Participate in a missionary experience that will help you confirm your calling and be sensitive to God's voice, understanding that He speaks in many ways. Be prepared to live the processes that God wants you to live, because they will be useful to you in the field. Surround yourself with people who recognize your calling, who contribute to your life with encouragement and confidence in God's promises and who see you as God sees you: as a clay vessel that He is forming for His glory".

Maritza Cumba

***

"It would have been impossible to carry out my missionary task without the support of so many people who during these seven years have been hand in hand with me, both in personal support and in the projects carried out. First of all, thanks to my parents, Griselle Lugo and Pedro Santiago. To my brothers, Juan Hernandez, Pedro D. Santiago, and Roberto Santiago. The love of my family, their acceptance of my call, their constant contribution to my support has been a comfort and joy to my life. Thanks to the Church of 1st Corinthians 13, who accepted to bless Honduras from their hearts, approximately 20 years ago. To our church, who in one way or another have moved heaven and earth so that we can work as missionaries with freedom. To the pastoral family, Pastors Pedro Montañez and Maria Avilez, Yeritza Montañez and

Miguel Rangel, Yina Montañez, Mariela Montañez and Jason Nery's; with whom we have accomplished so much.

To the AMIES Missionary Agency and its founder Luz Esther Cadiz. A great mentor and advisor. For being a neutral entity and for supporting us in difficult times.

To the churches Centro Cristiano Rescate, Pastors Monserrate and Josué Carrillo and Iglesia Centro Cristiano Vida Abundante. For believing in and helping me to support the AmaNacer Project. For helping me to bless so many mothers and their babies in extreme need.

To all those pastors, churches, projects, businesses, and people who have believed in the work that God has done through us and who allow us to reach out.

To all my Honduran brothers and sisters, who opened the doors of their land and their hearts to us. Thank you for allowing us to serve you. I will be eternally grateful."

Siris Santiago

***

"I want to thank: Costa Rican Evangelical Federation, Assemblies of God Missionary Agency of Costa Rica, Muslim Peoples International, the Churches that support us and our Family because they have always been by our side."

And I would like to take this space for a final word from me:

When we had been living in Indonesia for about three years, I started to think about everything that had happened in

Uzbekistan, the departure and how hard that episode was for us.   I remembered that when we left Costa Rica for Uzbekistan my husband and I said, let's take the coffin with us.   By that we meant that we were leaving with the idea of living and dying in that country, making our life there.   So, having to leave was very painful.   And then we were in Indonesia, three years have passed, how fast time went by!   Another country, I would never have imagined it, how incredible are the ways of the Lord.   As I thought about this moment I understood.   I remembered that when we left Uzbekistan the pain did not let me see the perfect plans that the Lord was laying out for my life.   But now, I can look back and see the beautiful picture the Lord had painted. That's how our life is, sometimes we can only see what we have in front of our eyes, but He has already drawn perfectly what is going to make our life a beautiful picture.   I understood that we had to go through what we went through to get there.   And I wouldn't change any of the experiences, no matter how painful they were, because He allowed me to get to this other town; to embrace and love other people; and because in all these processes of my life He has always been by my side."

Abigail Forero

***

"I praise our Heavenly Father for the life of each person who with love and joy have offered so that the extension of His kingdom on this earth continues to run among the people not yet reached and who to this day continue to sustain us, forming a great team.

I am very grateful for my sending church and my pastor who have always been aware of my life and work, and have always been attentive to every adventure that we have lived in this wonderful task.

Blessings and a huge hug."

Elba Bermudez

"I thank God first of all for allowing me to be part of His Master plan and to put my hands on "the plow." To my Church "Renacer, Una gran Familia en Cristo" of Cordoba, Argentina, and to the Pastoral Body, I give thanks, for sowing us in the nations, always giving us the care, support, ministerial and family support during these fifteen years. To Calvary City Church, Pastor Nino Gonzalez, the pastoral staff and the Missions Team of Orlando, FL, for being the church that welcomed us as adopted missionaries. To Rev. Diana E. Diana E. Barrera, director of missions of the Florida Multicultural District, for inviting me to be part of the missions team of this beautiful district as well as to participate in the COMHINA Central Florida table. To Pastor Claudia Bustamante and her tenacious challenge, friendship and modeling towards my ministerial life. To COMIBAM International, in the figure of Pastor Decio de Carvalho, giving me the opportunity to be part of the team leading the Intercession Department. To Wendy Colon, as director of Women in Missions for her patience in my absences due to overlapping ministry agendas. To each regional prayer leader for their friendship and responsibility in the task. I thank Jenny Oliphant, for challenging me to be part

of the Ethne Prayer Strategic Team, mobilizing prayer in Latin America.   To fellow field workers and friends who constantly enrich and nurture my life.

Finally, my special thanks to my family, my husband and daughter for understanding my commitments, schedules, and absences. Without their support I could not be effective in my ministerial task. I extend this last thanks to my extended family for their love, care, and constant prayerful support."

Mary Fernandez

***

"I thank God for having called me, for having chosen me to serve Him. His grace alone has sustained me all these years. I thank God for His faithfulness, for He has never left me, nor forsaken me. I thank God for my family and my local church who have always supported me unconditionally. I also thank God for those friends who have supported me and prayed for me throughout the years.   Finally, I thank God for the AMIES ministry, a ministry that He used to help me and guide me to fulfill the calling that God had given me.

For all of you who have read this book, I offer you the same word that God gave me from the day He called me for salvation, "Behold, I command you to be strong and courageous; do not be afraid or dismayed, for the LORD your God will be with you wherever you go." (Joshua 1:9)
God has given us the privilege of collaborating with Him, He has called us to be part of what He is doing in the nations. Let us strive, then, and put our hands to work, because the work in the Lord is not in vain and there are many people to reach. Let

us remember that we serve the one true God, the One who is, who was, and who is to come, and who has revealed to us the end of history: "After this I looked, and behold, a great multitude which no one could number, of all nations and tribes and peoples and tongues, standing before the throne and before the Lamb, clothed in white robes, with palm branches in their hands." (Revelation 7:9)
To Him be glory forever and ever, Amen!"

Amapola de la Peña

Acknowledgments

"I want to thank the collaboration of some people in the edition of this book that now everyone can enjoy: Pastor Victor Vazquez, Myriam Sanchez (retired teacher), my husband Rafael Amill (retired teacher), Rev. Luz Esther Cadiz, each one of the missionaries who sent their corrections. Thank you very much for the excellent work you did in such a short time.

To Rev. Luz Esther Cadiz, who accepted the challenge of writing the preface of this project of God. To all who prayed for this project for the glory of God, especially to my ministry partners in the Women in Missions Network of COMIBAM International and the sisters that God has given me who study with me at Wesley Seminary, Damaris, Claudia and Veronica, who committed to pray for this book and I know that God heard them.

God bless you all!"

About the cover

"I want to tell you something about the cover. When I had the name of the book I immediately thought of the cover as a landscape like the star of Bethlehem, the day Jesus was born. But such a photo was hard to find, if not impossible. A couple of days later the daughter of a friend who is a photographer had taken the photo that today is the cover of the book. In those days the comet Neowise was passing by, the brightest comet of the last seven years that could be observed with the naked eye from Earth. Coincidence, who knows, I don't think so, I think God himself gave me the photo and the cover. Well, the girl who took the photo was the same one who took the cover photo of another of my books, the one of my testimony, "Definitely Blind".

So, what better than the photo of the brightest comet for a book by the brightest, our God. Glory be to Him."

References

González, Justo L. & Carlos F. Cardoza. *Historia General de las Misiones.* España: Editorial Clie, 2008.

González, Justo L. & Zaida Maldonado Pérez. *Introducción a la Teología Cristiana.* Nashville: Adbington Press, 1998.

Poupard, Paul Cardinal. "Evangelio y Cultura: En los Umbrales del Tercer Milenio." Trabajo presentado, Universidad La Sapienza, Roma, 26 de mayo de 1998.

Protestante Digital, *El Evangelio vivido dentro de cada cultura.* Acceso el 10 de abril de 2020. https://protestantedigital.com/print/8580/El_Evangelio_vivido_dentro_de_cada_cultura